Developing a Successful Girls' and Women's Basketball Program

Stephenie Jordan

ISBN: 1-58518-522-1
Library of Congress Control Number: 2002102550

Book layout: Jeanne Hamilton
Cover design: Jennifer Bokelmann
Front cover photo: Andy Lyons/Allsport

Coaches Choice
P.O. Box 1828
Monterey, CA 93942
www.coacheschoice.com

ACKNOWLEDGMENTS

With sincere thanks and appreciation to

My Lord and Savior, Jesus Christ.

My husband, Jody, for his loving support and his coaching advice.

My parents, Roger and Claire Scott, for everything they do for us.

My son, Scott, for taking two-hour naps.

Ronda Ratcliff Norman, for saying, "You ought to write a book."

Trevor and Norma White, because I told them
I'd mention them in the book.

All of my former basketball players at
Bellville High School and Garrison High School.

CONTENTS

"The whistle sounded, the big ball was tossed into the air, Miss Ellsworth for Horace Mann whacked it aside to her sister forward, and for some minutes the floor was a whirlwind. The girls dashed hither and thither, tangled themselves in scrimmages, tumbled and picked themselves up, bent and swayed as joyously as ten-year-old children playing tag.

Eventually, a foul was called on Horace Mann, and Miss Vanderbilt took her place upon the line and tossed the ball plump into the net. Score, 1 for Montclair, and the spectators generously applauded."

Girls' basketball has certainly come a long way since the appearance of this article in *The New York Times* on March 4, 1897. The final score of the game was 10 - 5 and the headline read:

> "GIRLS PLAY BASKETBALL: It Was the First Match Game of the Winning Team—Losers Chewed Gum—The Pastime Recommended as Teaching Restraint."

The losers chewed gum? Anyway, the game went from peach baskets as goals and losers chewing gum to a six-player version of the game in which offensive and defensive players were restricted to one half of the court. That version, too (in the late 1970s), was replaced by the game we know now: full-court action in which young women demonstrate well-developed skills and fast-paced play. I did, however, coach an eighth-grade girls' team to a 5-4 victory (yes, five points to four points) in which the only skills exhibited were turnovers and air balls. But a win is a win, right?

So what's this book all about? If you're like me, you're always searching for ways to improve your program and you'll buy as many books as it takes to find just one good idea. This book will be the last you need to buy. It is a resource-packed, comprehensive handbook that touches on more than the X's and O's of the sport. Many areas left untouched by other basketball books are covered here, including try-out procedures, job descriptions for your assistants, game-day considerations, and much more.

I found that there was a great need for something besides another drill book (although they are very helpful), so I decided to start from square one. Chapter 1 will take you through scheduling your season up to the first day of practice. The next two chapters will give you insight into planning the season, having try-outs, the components of a good practice, and a sample practice schedule. Chapters 4 through 7 are related specifically to the X's and O's of coaching women's basketball and include offensive plays, drills for practice, and special plays for "crunch time." The scouting chapter includes charts, forms, and questions to ask when evaluating your opponent. Chapter 9 is dedicated to game day considerations, including how to develop a game plan, what to take to an away game, coaching points during the game, and how to deal with the press. Program management wouldn't be complete without dealing with an off-season program. Chapter 11 explains how to plan your off-season, including suggested activities to use, a rating system for the athletes, a sample 10-week program, and a summer workout program.

Finally, I've included three special sections in the Appendix: Planning a Tournament, Organizing a Youth Program, and Fund-Raising Ideas. The sections are in a timeline format and take you from the planning stages to the day of the event and after.

Developing a Successful Girls' and Women's Basketball Program is intended for use as a reference. Pick and choose what you need when you need it. I hope you find it gives you the added edge you need to be a successful coach.

A Preseason Checklist

BEFORE THE FIRST DAY OF PRACTICE

- ❏ Inventory current equipment
- ❏ Make a needs/wants list for the athletic director
- ❏ Filling out a purchase order form
- ❏ Order equipment
- ❏ Send letters to athletes
- ❏ Make calls to players
- ❏ Schedule season
- ❏ Make schedules and distribute
- ❏ Request checks for tournaments
- ❏ Secure officials
- ❏ Fill out travel requests
- ❏ Get CDL and bus driving certification
- ❏ Research radio coverage
- ❏ Develop team rules and policies

- ❏ Meet with prospective team members
- ❏ Schedule a parent meeting
- ❏ Choose a motivational theme
- ❏ Prepare themes for the week
- ❏ Order team shirts
- ❏ Make signs for businesses
- ❏ Make an attendance board
- ❏ Pick music for the dressing room
- ❏ Set media day
- ❏ Post goal charts
- ❏ Check video equipment
- ❏ Get a coaches packet ready
- ❏ Issue equipment
- ❏ Organize yourself

❏ Inventorying equipment

To develop a list of needs and wants, you'll need to know what you've got. If you just got the job, don't rely on the list left by the previous coach. You'll need to see for yourself just what's stuffed in that closet, and it will probably need to be reorganized. Figure 1.1 illustrates a sample form that can be useful to record the equipment.

Anywhere Independent School District
Women's Basketball Inventory 2001-2002

Item Description	New	Usable	Old	Total	Needed

Figure 1.1. Inventory sheet.

❑ Making a needs and wants list

If you want some items that may be out of the ordinary, then do what you can to make a professional presentation to your athletic director. For example, if you think you can't live without a specific ball rack, then find three companies that make them, find the best price, and show you've done your homework. If he/she rejects the idea, then begin thinking about a fund-raiser (see Appendix C).

Among the items you should include in your needs list are the following:

- Shoes – Order new shoes for your high school squads and pass hand-me-downs to your junior high teams. If you don't have enough to pass down, give your junior high athletes the option to purchase theirs through the same company.

- Uniforms – Make sure you have enough to fit everyone – not just clothe everyone. Some players may not fit into those 1985 uniforms your teams are still wearing. You want your team to look good and feel comfortable.

- Practice uniforms – Issue these the first day you meet and make everyone wear them. When everyone dresses the same you have a sense of team. No telling what they'll come out in if you leave it up to them. Also, a trick I once learned from a colleague is to outfit your team in sweatpants. It keeps their legs warm, avoiding strains and pulls, and it gives them a particular mind-set. Once the sweatpants come off and the uniform goes on, they know it's game time. It's purely psychological but it's effective.

- Basketballs – Buy as many basketballs as your budget allows and set two aside for home games. If you plan to advance beyond district, find out what kind of balls will be provided and buy some. This could give your team an edge.

- Pinnies – Sharing pinnies is not a pleasant experience, so order enough for everyone. Consider ordering four different colors so the junior varsity and varsity or seventh- and eighth-grade players have enough for intersquad scrimmages.

- Videotapes – The football coach or athletic director may be ordering these in bulk. If not, add these to your list.

- Whistles and lanyards – Get two or three. They are easy to misplace.

- Athletic training supplies – The only two words you need to know about 90% of the injuries you'll see are "ice it." Hopefully you will have a trainer on staff who can deal with serious knee problems or severe strains and pulls. Otherwise, learn how to tape an ankle. For some, ankle injuries are a "chronic problem" (especially in junior high where some players seem to love the attention). Get a slip-on brace for these individuals so they feel important and you can avoid taping 20 ankles every day. Among the items that you should consider ordering for your medicine kit are the following:

Adhesive tape	Heel cups (plastic)
Pre-wrap material	Instant cold packs
Bandages/band-aids (assorted sizes)	Internal agents (Tylenol, ibuprofen, aspirin)
Butterfly strips	
Sterile pads (2″ x 2″s and 3″ x 3″s)	Peroxide
Elastic knee sleeves (S, M, & L)	Safety pins
Elastic thigh sleeves (S, M, & L)	Scissors
Eyewash	Tape adherent (spray can)
Feminine napkins	Tape cutters
Gauze (1-inch and 2-inch rolls)	Tweezers

❑ **Filling out a purchase order form**

If your business office doesn't already have a purchase order form that it employs, Figure 1.2 offers an example of a form that you could use.

❑ **Ordering equipment**

When ordering equipment, write down the representative's name, phone number, and the date and time you placed your order. If there is a mistake in the order, you will have a contact person. Make copies of the purchase order requests and compare invoices of shipped items with your list. Highlight items as they arrive.

❑ **Sending letters to athletes**

The letter sent to athletes should include any important dates before the first day of practice. Figure 1.3 illustrates an example of a letter that could be sent to prospective players.

❑ **Making calls to players**

Get a list from your school's administrative office with the telephone numbers of your prospective athletes and call all of them. Be sure to personally speak to the athlete instead of getting information from the parents. Simply ask her if she will be playing basketball this year. If she says "no," then encourage her to at least come out and see if she likes it, and let her know you would enjoy seeing her participate. If she will be playing, get her shirt, short, and shoe size for uniform ordering purposes.

PURCHASE REQUEST FORM

Date:
Requested by:
Approved by:
Purchase Order #:

Quantity	Catalogue #	Description	Unit Price	Total
			REQUISITION TOTAL	

Figure 1.2. Sample purchase request form.

❏ Scheduling the season

If you have an experienced team, find challenging opponents for your pre-district play. Otherwise, find some weaker teams to build some confidence as you approach district or conference play. Remember to designate one game for parents' night and another for an interleague youth night (preferably at games where you need extra support). Once you have your schedule in place, print a nice copy and distribute it to everyone who needs one (players, principals, officials, athletic director, etc.).

❏ Requesting checks for tournaments

Simply fill out a check request form (obtained from your business office or athletic office) and submit it to your athletic director as soon as possible.

Dear Prospective Basketball Player,

I hope this finds your school year/summer going well. The following list includes some important information about meetings, practice times, and other dates of interest.

DATE	EVENT	LOCATION	TIME
Sept. 4	Physicals	Field House	3:00 - 6:00 pm
Sept. 12	Parent and team meeting	Cafeteria	7:00 pm
Oct. 23	First day of practice	Old Gym	3:30 - 5:30 pm
Nov. 1	Media day	New Gym	5:00 pm
Nov. 3	Meet the team	New Gym	5:30 pm
	Intersquad Scrimmage		
Nov. 7	Scrimmage vs. Team X	There	5:00 pm

Hope you are having a great summer. I look forward to seeing you on Sept. 12.

Sincerely,

Coach Jordan

Figure 1.3. Sample letter to athletes.

❏ Securing officials

Send a copy of your schedule to the secretary of the officials' chapter you have chosen and check at least the day before your game to make sure you'll have officials at your game. If it is your responsibility to fill out the official's pay sheets after each game, get them from the athletic director or use the form in Figure 1.4 as an example.

❏ Filling out travel requests

Under normal circumstances, the transportation director at your school will insist on having at least three days notice in order to provide transportation for your team. Get as many forms as you'll need for all of your out-of-town games and fill them all out at once. Once you've turned them all in, just check with the director a few days in advance to make sure your bus/van will be ready.

❏ Getting CDL and bus driving certification

This is not a requirement for everyone, but needs mentioning. Your state's Department of Motor Vehicles or Department of Public Safety will issue your commercial drivers license (CDL). The bus driving certification can be obtained through a local school

```
ANYWHERE INDEPENDENT SCHOOL DISTRICT
              INVOICE FOR FEES
         PAID TO BASKETBALL OFFICIALS


    Date: _____        Number of games: _____


    ❑ Varsity  ❑ Junior Varsity  ❑ 9th Grade  ❑ 8th Grade  ❑ 7th Grade


OFFICIAL'S INFORMATION:

Name: _____ SS# _____

Address: _____

    ┌─────────────────────┐        ┌──────────────────────┐
    │     PAY SCALE        │        │   NUMBER OF GAMES     │
    │  1 game    $17.00    │        │       WORKED          │
    │                      │        │   ❑  1 game           │
    │  2 games   $35.00    │        │   ❑  2 games          │
    │  3 games   $60.00    │        │   ❑  3 games          │
    └─────────────────────┘        └──────────────────────┘

Total mileage _____ @0.28 per mile = $ _____

Fee due for officiating         = $ _____

Total due                       = $ _____
```

Figure 1.4. Sample official's pay sheet.

district and is usually offered during the summer. For example, initial certification in Texas is a 20-hour course. A refresher is necessary every three years to maintain certification.

❑ Researching radio coverage

Find a local or semi-local radio station, and ask if they would cover a few of your games. It doesn't hurt to ask — especially if they cover football games in the area. Why not women's basketball?

❑ Developing team rules and policies

The athletic director will probably have guidelines and rules for the entire athletic program. You will certainly have to adhere to those policies but if you are given the liberty to create your own, consider these general fundamental areas that may need clarification and address them to fit your personal situation:

- Classroom expectations
- Alcohol and drug violations
- Stealing
- Lettering
- Travel to and from games
- Attendance
- Excused and unexcused absences
- Profanity
- Quitting the team
- Injury or illness
- Unsportsmanlike conduct
- Dress code
- Equipment management
- Multiple extracurricular athletes
- Suspension from school
- Disrespect to teachers and coaches
- Dressing room behavior
- General behavior – 13 tips:
  - ✓ Replace "uh-huh" and "naw, huh" with "yes, ma'am," "no, ma'am," yes, sir," and "no, sir."
  - ✓ Maintain your composure.
  - ✓ Do a good job in the classroom.
  - ✓ Hustle at all times.
  - ✓ Do not argue with teammates.
  - ✓ Do not argue with officials.
  - ✓ Do not swear.
  - ✓ Do not sulk. If you have a problem or think you are being mistreated, see the coach.
  - ✓ Maintain a first-class appearance.
  - ✓ Do not have temper tantrums. Do not throw balls or equipment of any kind during practices or games.
  - ✓ Practice good manners in class, on campus, and on road trips, as well as in your community. Be a first-class individual.

✓ Be on time.

✓ Have *faith* in yourself, your team, and your coaches. Be willing to sacrifice to be the best you can be.

- Demerit system — As a former cheerleader sponsor, I was introduced to the demerit system and feel it can be very useful for an athletic program as well. Assign point values for violations of the team policies and time-based point totals for further disciplinary action. For example, once an athlete receives five points (or demerits), the athlete incurs a one-game suspension. However, if an athlete goes one week without getting any points, one point is deducted from her total. If the athlete accumulates 15 points during the season, she is expelled from the team. Some examples of how points may be assigned include:

✓ Suspension from school = five points

✓ Cheating or any other academic dishonesty = four points

✓ Unexcused absence from basketball practice = three points

✓ Unexcused absence from leadership council meeting = three points

✓ Unexcused absence from class = three points

✓ Unexcused absence from tutorials = two points

✓ Dress code violations = one point

✓ Dressing room violations = one point

✓ Failure to follow instructions = one point

❑ **Meeting with prospective team members**

Pass out your program handbook and go over each item in detail. Among the items the handbook should include are the following:

- School history – Include team records, individual records (high point game, etc.), names of players who went on to play collegiate ball, and former award winners

- Season schedule

- Maps to schools for out-of-town games (www.mapquest.com is a good place to start)

- School requirements for participation

- Team rules and policies

- Information on equipment issued by the school and what the athlete should provide

- Criteria for earning a varsity letter

- Phone numbers of school and coaching staff

- Self-evaluation: You and I desire a program and team of which we can be proud. This includes giving our best and acting with dignity. If we do these things, the winning will take care of itself. We want people to say that the young people of our school are a "first-class group." If you are not sure what "class" is, ask yourself the following questions:

  ✓ If I don't make first team, am I still willing to work and support the team during games and practice?

  ✓ Do I treat teachers with respect?

  ✓ Am I polite to everyone I meet?

  ✓ Do I use obscene and abusive language as a major part of my vocabulary?

  ✓ Do I make excuses for my mistakes and shortcomings, or do I accept the responsibility and strive to improve?

  ✓ Do I follow training rules to the letter, or do I have the attitude of "what the coach doesn't know, can't hurt me"?

  ✓ When I am feeling down and having a bad day, do I still try to be a good influence on my teammates?

  ✓ When there is a problem, do I try to help solve it, or do I become part of the problem?

  If you can honestly answer these questions with a positive response, then you truly have class. If you cannot, then now is the time to start in the right direction. In many cases, when other factors are equal, the outcome of a contest may be decided by the team with the most class.

- Commitment page — The last page of your handbook should include a summary of what you expect and a place for the athlete's signature and the signatures of the athlete's parents. Figure 1.5 illustrates an example of a sample commitment form.

❏ Scheduling a parent meeting

Notify the local newspaper well in advance and include the date of the meeting in your letter to the athletes. Your parent meeting should address the following subjects:

I. Introduction

- Your background

- Success you've had as a coach (or anticipated success)

II. Explanation of Philosophy

- Conduct of athletes:

THE COMMITMENT TO EXCELLENCE

I have read the handbook and understand the policies of the basketball program and the athletic program.

In addition to keeping the aforementioned policies, I will:

- Follow all school rules, district rules, and UIL rules;
- Strive to excel academically;
- Not lie or steal;
- Not use alcohol, illegal drugs, tobacco, or other harmful substances; and,
- Give my best effort at all times.

I hereby state that I have received, read, and understand the policies and agree to abide by these policies in all respects.

Student Signature: _____

Parent/Guardian Signature: _____

Date: _____

Figure 1.5. Sample policies commitment form.

    ✓ Class, character, commitment to excellence

    ✓ Train hard to become active contributors to society

    ✓ Alcohol and drug violations – punishment involved

- Academics:

    ✓ Tutoring program

    ✓ Grade checks

- Keys to success:

    ✓ Mental attitude

    ✓ Developing winning potential

    ✓ Athletes will be prepared

- Multi-extracurricular athletes:

    ✓ Athletes will be involved in extracurricular activities

    ✓ Conflicting schedules will be resolved by coach, teacher, and student

III. Discipline

- Disrespect to teachers and coaches:
    - ✓ Conditioning program will be administered
    - ✓ Behavior agreement (Figure 1.6 illustrates an example of a form that can be used)
- Alcohol and drug violations:
    - ✓ First offense
    - ✓ Second offense
    - ✓ Third offense
- Missed practices:
    - ✓ Excused
    - ✓ Unexcused

IV. Closing – Question and Answer Time

BEHAVIOR AGREEMENT

Dear_____ ,

I want to apologize for the way I've been acting in your class. Because of my poor behavior, Coach Jordan has put me in a reminder program until you decide my behavior has improved. Once you feel it has improved, please sign this sheet and return it to Coach Jordan.

Thank you very much,   Instructor: _____
                                                              signature

_____   _____
                                                           printed name

Date: _____   Date: _____

Figure 1.6. Sample behavior agreement form.

❏ Choosing a motivational theme

Motivation can be an integral part in the success of your team. Choose a theme that can be represented by something tangible and give that tangible item to each athlete, for example, a rope, a nail, a star, a match, etc. You have to decide how it relates to your team as a motivational tool.

❏ Preparing themes for the week

In addition to a special theme, spend some time each week emphasizing a certain character trait (courage, loyalty, boldness, decisiveness, dependability, etc.) and decorate the locker room with quotes that correspond to the weekly trait. The signs can be done on a computer by your managers and can be posted on lockers, doors, and bulletin boards.

❏ Ordering team shirts

What you have printed on the team shirts could correlate with the motivational theme you've chosen, or you might purchase ready-made shirts.

❏ Making signs for businesses

To generate some excitement within the community, make signs that offer some special proclamation, for example, "I'm a Lady (*Mascot*) Basketball Backer!" This step may give you an opportunity to personally meet prominent people in the community.

❏ Making an attendance board

A simple method of keeping track of a large number of athletes is to make an attendance board out of plywood, nails, and tags. Write each athlete's name on both sides of a tag – one side in black and the other in red (or a school color). Put an appropriate number of nails on a piece of plywood and hang the tags. Each athlete simply turns her tag over according to the day (black or red). Station a manager or coach by the board so athletes don't flip someone else's tag.

❏ Picking music for the dressing room

Make a tape (or entrust this to your managers who are probably more attuned to your player's musical tastes than you are) to be played while the girls are dressing before practice. If you're really creative, find a song that goes with your theme and make it "the song" of the season.

❏ Setting media day

Picture day should obviously be after your season begins. It is important to schedule a photographer well in advance.

❑ Posting goal charts

You might post several different goal charts, corresponding to your priorities. Figure 1.7 offers an example of a sample goal chart.

TEAM GOALS

	Game 1	Game 2	Game 3	Game 4	Game 5	Game 6
Assists						
Off. Rebounds						
Def. Rebounds						
Steals						
Field Goal %						
Free Throw %						
Charges						
Blocked Shots						
Fouls						
Turnovers						

STEPS TO THE PLAYOFFS

STATE

etc.

Quitman

Mineola

Mt. Vernon

Figure 1.7. Sample goal chart.

❑ Checking video equipment

You'll want to have your games videotaped, so check on your equipment before the first game. You may have to check out a camcorder from the library if the athletic department doesn't have one for the women's program.

❑ Getting a coaches packet ready

Include the following items in your coaches packets:

- Agenda for meeting:

Sample Agenda

7:30   Introductions of coaches

7:40   Philosophy of coaching:

    ✓   Expectations

    ✓   Discipline of athletes

    ✓   Attitude

8:00   Job descriptions

8:20   Offensive introduction

10:00 Break

10:10 Defensive introduction

11:30 Staff discussion:

    ✓   Missed practices

    ✓   Senior leadership

    ✓   Motivation

    ✓   Pre-game

    ✓   Grades

    ✓   Attendance

    ✓   Team policies

    ✓   Other

12:00 Dismiss

- Job descriptions:

The following examples illustrate the assigned duties for a typical staff of four high school coaches (head coach and three assistants) and two junior high coaches.

COACH #1

- ✓ Assist the varsity head coach with practices and in games.
- ✓ Assist the head coach with college recruiting.
- ✓ Wash coordinator — assign this task to managers.
- ✓ Plan and procure meals for all out-of-town games.
- ✓ Call in scores and stats after each game.
- ✓ Prepare the end-of-season report for all levels.
- ✓ Post the computer printout of individual and team stats after each game.
- ✓ Coordinate academic and tutorial programs.
- ✓ Keep track of videotapes.
- ✓ Put a list in teachers' boxes three days prior to out-of-town trips.
- ✓ Compile a needs list for purchasing.
- ✓ Oversee maintenance of gym.
- ✓ Manage travel-request and return-travel forms.
- ✓ Develop an in-season and off-season weight program.
- ✓ Schedule officials, clock keeper, and scorekeeper for home games.
- ✓ Keep a stat sheet during varsity games.
- ✓ Perform evening and after-athletics lock-up.

COACH #2

- ✓ Assist the head coach during games.
- ✓ Act as the head junior varsity coach.
- ✓ Give out locker and lock assignments.
- ✓ Maintain all lists, for example, telephone, locker, combinations, ID#'s.
- ✓ Coordinate use of equipment.
- ✓ Submit inventory request and keep up-to-date records on all equipment.
- ✓ Maintain a neat and orderly equipment room.
- ✓ Make sure that players do not wear equipment home.

- ✓ Submit an inventory of equipment two weeks after season is over.
- ✓ Manage roll check, board, and record for office.
- ✓ Supervise managers – grades, duties during practice and games, out-of-town checkout.
- ✓ Assist with academics.
- ✓ Set up gym 30 minutes before practice.
- ✓ Supervise locker room.
- ✓ Secure game ball at home games when game is over.
- ✓ Collect unclaimed equipment from the bench when game is over.
- ✓ Pick up scorebook when the game is over.

COACH #3

- ✓ Assist the varsity head coach during games.
- ✓ Act as head freshman coach.
- ✓ Coordinate scouting.
- ✓ Make and print team rosters (include number, name, position, classification).
- ✓ Oversee storage, care, and maintenance of video equipment.
- ✓ Manage the care and prevention of injuries.
- ✓ Keep files on all athletes – physicals, medical history, emergency numbers, etc.
- ✓ Submit a needs list of medical items at the end of the season.
- ✓ Manage all strength testing, charts, workout cards, and motivational record boards.
- ✓ Handle game-day pack-up – balls, charts, clipboards, water, cups, towels, scorebook.
- ✓ Keep a shot chart during varsity games.
- ✓ Ensure that gym is set up for home games.
- ✓ Make sure that video equipment gets to and from games, including extension cords, camera, and tapes.
- ✓ Assist with student academics.
- ✓ Set up the gym 30 minutes before practice.
- ✓ Supervise locker-room activities.

JUNIOR HIGH COACHES

- ✓ Plan the daily practice schedule for junior high athletes.
- ✓ Monitor academics of junior high athletes.
- ✓ Maintain attendance list, including ID#'s.
- ✓ Take care of early dismissals for out-of-town trips; put list in teachers' boxes three days prior to trip.
- ✓ Type team rosters and have them ready to be distributed at the games.
- ✓ Provide game-summary report to high school varsity coach by 8:00 a.m. following game day.
- ✓ Manage roll check, board, and record; report to high school varsity coach daily.
- ✓ Oversee equipment issue and inventory records; coordinate needs with high school program.
- ✓ Organize junior high parent meeting; notify high school varsity coach when it will be held.
- ✓ Set up the gym 30 minutes before practice.
- ✓ Supervise locker-room activities.
- ✓ Make sure locker rooms are available.
- ✓ Oversee wash schedule with trainer.

- Program policies
- Academic plan (explained fully later in this chapter)
- Offensive and defensive system

❏ **Issuing equipment**

Each assistant coach may come up with her own equipment checkout chart. Figure 1.8 illustrates an example of a sheet that can be employed in this regard.

❏ **Organizing yourself**

Keep a notebook dedicated to basketball only, and divide it into the following sections:

- Schedules — Include your team's schedule and a copy of each conference opponent's schedule.
- Roster and eligibility forms — Before the season begins, have each athlete fill out an information card with her name, address, phone number, birth date,

2002-2003 Basketball Season Equipment Checkout Sheet				
Name	Shirt #	Shorts #	Shoe size	Returned

Figure 1.8. Sample equipment checkout sheet.

shoe size, pant size, and shirt size. After your manager types it in alphabetically, put your copy in the notebook. Include any eligibility forms you may need as well.

- Inventory sheet
- Bus requests — Put a copy of each request in this section so if a mix-up occurs, you'll have documentation.
- Purchase orders — Use your purchase orders to check off equipment as it arrives. These forms can be used to help with inventory record keeping as well.

- Important phone numbers — List the name and phone number of the person at 'your officials' chapter you'll need to call if an official doesn't show. Also, list the names and numbers of each coach of each team you will be playing in case you need to get in touch with them.

- District/conference notes and rules — Once a week, the chairperson of the district usually sends results to each coach with team standings and scores. Include any rule changes or other pertinent information about the district or conference.

- Workout notes — Compile a master list of skills and situations for your sport. Keep your workout notes so that every area is covered. These notes can be a valuable tool for next year as well.

- Drills — As you find drills you like, either from this book, other books, the Internet, journals, or clinics, make copies and put them in yourfolder for easy reference. You may want to categorize your drills into sub-sections (e.g. shooting, dribbling, free throws, etc.).

AFTER PRACTICE BEGINS

- ❏ Vote on leadership council
- ❏ Make a media guide
- ❏ Get an academic plan ready
- ❏ Choose a manager
- ❏ Train a videographer
- ❏ Send thank you notes to parents
- ❏ Recognize honor roll students
- ❏ Visit the elementary schools

❏ Voting on a leadership council

As adults and coaches, we are more knowledgeable than our athletes. On the other hand, we still need to listen to them. A good way to do this is to have your team vote for members of a leadership council. This council should be comprised not just with your team captains, but also with a fair number of representatives from the team to meet with you on a weekly basis to just talk about "things." Although they may or may not have legitimate gripes, the council is a good way to really stay in touch with your team. During the off-season, take this leadership council to visit other schools that have successful programs and let your athletes see what other teams are doing to prepare for the next season. Let them see how hard those teams are working, and then your athletes will realize they can work harder and that what they are doing now will pay off later.

❏ Making a media guide

This guide can be as simple or elaborate as you like. Most football teams have them made and include pictures of all the players and coaches, a roster, and a schedule. Their format can be used as a guide.

❑ Getting an academic plan ready

Whether or not your state has a strict rule about passing classes before being eligible to play, teachers appreciate the interest you take in the academic success of your athletes. After all, without academics, there would be no extracurricular activities. The following six-step procedure can be employed to monitor the academic progress of your athletes.

- STEP #1: Type a list of all participating athletes on one sheet using columns and a small font if necessary. Figure 1.9 illustrates an example of a sheet that can be used in this regard.

Teachers,

I would like to implement a weekly grade check for the basketball players to ensure their academic success. As a coaching staff, we will work with you and help with discipline as well as tutoring, if necessary.

Please look over the following list, circle any basketball players you have in class, add any that aren't on this list, and return it to Coach Jordan's box by Friday afternoon. This will be the last time you will have to sort through the entire roster. You will have an individualized sheet starting Monday or Tuesday. Thanks for your help.

Coach Jordan

Aschenbeck, Amy	Lach, Lisa	Schmidt, Stacy
Baker, Paige	Lightner, Paige	Schmidt, Tiffany
Banks, Pam	Lopez, Dory	Skillern, Kathy
Barrett, Mindy	Marsten, Cathy	Smart, Mece
Bost, Kristen	Merkel, Leslie	Smith, Tammy
Corley, Casey	O'Canas, Shelby	Smitheal, Amanda
Cranford, Denise Beth	Pilcik, Amanda	Sotello, Sheri
Gwin, Teresa	Pond, Joellen	Waddle, Liz
Hawkins, Gloria	Rivers, Gwen	Yawn, Mickey
Hernandez, Carmen	Rusnak, Belinda	

Figure 1.9. Sample sheet for listing players for the school's teachers.

- STEP #2: Distribute this list to each teacher and ask them to circle the name of any players they have in their class and then to return it to you (or your box). Keep a master list of all teachers who have turned in their sheets and track down those who haven't.

Lady Wildcat Weekly Grade Report

Teacher: Beicker, Cathy

Week of: August 14 - 18

Please check the list and make necessary changes (add or delete names). Then, complete the form and return it to Coach Jordan's box by Thursday morning. We would like to meet with you if you have a student-athlete who is failing (or nearly failing) or has been a discipline problem. Thanks for your support.

NAME	GRADE PASS/FAIL/ BORDERLINE (70-75)	BEHAVIOR EXCELLENT SATISFACTORY UNSATISFACTORY	COMMENTS
	P F B	E S U	
	P F B	E S U	
	P F B	E S U	
	P F B	E S U	
	P F B	E S U	
	P F B	E S U	
	P F B	E S U	
	P F B	E S U	
	P F B	E S U	
	P F B	E S U	
	P F B	E S U	
	P F B	E S U	
	P F B	E S U	
	P F B	E S U	

ADDITIONAL COMMENTS:

Figure 1.10. Sample weekly grade report form.

- STEP #3: Once you have each teacher's list, type individual reports for each teacher listing only those athletes that they have in class. It requires some work to get this in place but it makes it easier on the teachers. Figure 1.10 shows an example of a sample weekly grade report form.

- STEP #4: After the first grade check, compile all the information into one report and divide the number of athletes with academic problems among your coaches. Each coach should speak directly to the teacher and work on improving the student's situation. Figure 1.11 shows a sample summary report form that can be used in this regard.

Teacher's Name	Student Name	Grade	Behavior	Comments
Beicker, Cathy		P	U	Talks excessively in class. Good student though.
	Stacy Schmidt	B	E	Hasn't turned in two papers.
	Paige Baker	P	U	
	Amy Aschenbeck	P	U	Sleeps in class on occasion.
Bryant, Roger	Julie Simpson	B	U	Tends to disrupt and talk excessively.
	Mindy Barrett	B	S	Needs to make up a test.

Figure 1.11. Sample summary report form.

- STEP #5: Be sure to also keep up with the athletes that are doing well. Recognize honor roll students by posting a sign on their lockers, on the bulletin board, or in the gym.

- STEP #6: Prepare a report to be presented to the school board during each grading period. Determine each player's grade point average for each team and then present the following information: number of A's, B's, C's, D's, and F's; team GPAs; all A's honor roll members; A's and B's honor roll members; and any incompletes. If you want to get fancy, graph this information using Excel. Include a cover sheet as well. Figure 1.12 illustrates an example of how this information can be organized and presented.

❑ Choosing a manager

The most valuable people you can have on your staff are responsible, trustworthy, and willing student managers. After the season begins and some participants realize that the sport is just not for them, consider asking them to stay with the team and become managers. Give them a job description so they know exactly what will be expected of them.

Women's Basketball Grade Report
Weeks 1-6

Varsity GPAs

90 - 100	7/30	23%
80 - 89	21/30	70%
70 - 79	2/30	7%

TEAM GPA: 87

Junior Varsity GPAs

90 - 100	7/39	18%
80 - 89	28/39	72%
70 - 79	3/39	8%
Incompletes	1/39	2%

TEAM GPA: 86

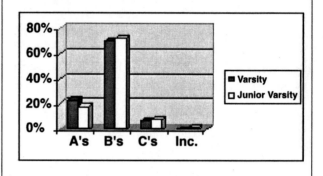

A's Honor Roll

Varsity	3/30	10%
Junior Varsity	0/39	0%
Total Program	3/69	4%

A's/B's Honor Roll

Varsity	7/30	23%
Junior Varsity	8/39	21%
Total Program	15/69	22%

Failures and Incompletes

Varsity	1/30	3%
Junior Varsity	3/39	6%
Total Program	4/69	6%

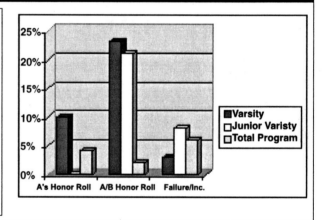

Figure 1.12. Sample school board report.

MANAGER DUTIES AND EXPECTATIONS

General:

- Attend all practices and games.
- Be willing and ready to do any tasks that are asked of you.
- Stay positive and give that impression to the coach.
- Never complain about anything asked of you.
- Be organized and efficient at the games.
- Act like you know what you're doing and ask for help only when necessary.
- Assist the team and coach whenever you can.

At games:

- After arrival, go to the bathroom and take care of business.
- Fill out scoring book and stat sheets and have ready for the game.
- Fill water bottles as soon as you can.
- Set balls and towels out for team before they start warming up.
- Find out where you will be sitting and try to stay there so you're available.
- If you have any questions during the game, ask the other team's manager first. If that individual can't help and the matter can't wait, ask the coach.
- Make sure the scoring book is correct after the game. If needed, compare with the other team's book.

At practices:

- Wash towels and uniforms.
- Summarize stats and put into computer.
- Clean up and organize any rooms that need it.
- Ask the coach if there are any specific jobs that need to be done.
- Make inspiring signs for the locker room.
- If time allows, replace material on bulletin boards.
- Help team and coaches as needed.

❏ Training a videographer

One of the managers can be designated as videographer as long as she knows exactly how you'd like the game filmed. Some tips to ensure a good videotape include:

- Video cameras normally rewind a small amount each time the camera is turned off or paused. Let at least three to five seconds run off the tape before you stop. This will eliminate erasing good footage. It also takes about the same amount of time when beginning to record after the camera has been turned off. Since plenty of tape exists for the game, be liberal as you start and stop filming.
- Try to set up and film from a nice, high place in the middle of the gym so you're out of everyone's way.
- Scan the gym floor slowly using a wide-angle shot, occasionally zooming in on the action. If you have to move the camera to follow the ball, zoom back out.
- Keep the camera on a tripod to avoid shaking the camera. Don't talk while filming —this will record sound.

- If you are not set up in the middle, always zoom in when the action is at the far end of the gym. Keep both sidelines in view — no closer.

- Zoom back out as the action approaches you so you can keep all the action in the frame. During time-outs, film the players, coaches, and fans so this footage can be used for the end-of-year video.

- Label the tape with the opponent's name, the date, and the final score of the game.

❏ Sending thank you notes to parents

You might think this is a corny idea and not worth your time, but I can assure you that some parents will appreciate it. Playing involves not just a sacrifice for the athlete, but also for her entire family, and thanking the parents for their support is important.

❏ Recognizing honor roll students

At each grading period, encourage the principal or athletic director to recognize the athletes that have done well in their academics. Promoting their accomplishments may also encourage other athletes to do better in class.

CHAPTER 2

Planning the Season

PLAYER ASSESSMENT

Have a try-out at the beginning of the season to assess the skills of your players. Although you may have an idea who will make the team, ranking your players will give everyone a fair chance. Some of the following drills and tests can be employed to evaluate a player's performance:

- Shooting drills
- Ball-handling drills
- Dribbling drills
- Passing drills
- Agility drills

- Explosion test
- Endurance test
- 1-on-1 half-court games
- 3-on-3 half-court games
- 5-on-5 full-court scrimmage

A FORMULA FOR EVALUATION

Once you have determined the skills you would like to evaluate, put the numbers in the "formula" you have developed to rank your players. Personally, I prefer to use the same scale as track meets but you can assign points however you'd like.

Whether or not you want to post the results of your evaluation efforts for the players to see is up to you. It may be a good motivational technique to use throughout the year or you may choose to use this information for personal use in determining how to organize your teams. It also may become useful if a parent absolutely believes their child should be a starter on varsity. The following example illustrates how you can undertake the evaluative process.

TIMED EVENTS

- STEP #1: Take ten percent of the best time. This percentage enables you to add a fair amount of time regardless of the length of time of each event. As the time for different events gets longer (e.g. the two-mile run), the range gets longer.

- STEP #2: Add the result of step #1 to the best time to determine a range.

  ❑ Example: Full-court speed dribble

  ❑ Best time = 11.2

  ❑ Take 11.2 x 0.10 = 1.1 (rounded to nearest tenth)

  ❑ Add 1.1 to the best time (11.2 + 1.1 = 12.3) to get the range for ten points. The chart illustrated in Figure 2.1 can be used for the entire scale.

SKILL EVENTS

- STEP #1: Take the best attempt and assign it ten points.
- STEP #2: The next best attempt gets eight points, etc.

  ❑ Example: Lay-ups

  ❑ Best attempt = 12

  ❑ Or assign points according to number of attempts (13 baskets = 13 points). The chart illustrated in Figure 2.2 can be used as an example of how to assign points for skill events.

11.2 to 12.3 = 10 points
12.4 to 13.5 = 8 points
13.6 to 14.7 = 6 points
14.8 to 15.9 = 4 points
16.0 to 17.1 = 2 points
17.2 to 18.3 = 1 point

12 = 10 points
11 = 8 points
10 = 6 points
9 = 4 points
8 = 2 points

Figure 2.1. Sample of a timed event chart.   Figure 2.2. Sample of a skill event chart.

EXPLANATION OF EVENTS

SHOOTING DRILLS

- Lay-ups (L.U.) – Set two cones at each elbow of the lane. To start the drill, the clock is set for one minute, and the player, with ball in hand, stands on the outside of the right-hand cone. At the whistle, she dribbles to the basket, shoots a right-handed lay-up, retrieves the ball, dribbles around the left-hand cone, and shoots a left-handed lay-up. The drill repeats for one minute. Refer to Figure 2.3.

- Hot-shot spots (Ht.Sht.) – Mark seven spots on the floor in front of the three-point line but outside the key. A player to rebound will be needed for the shooter. The shooter starts at point A, shoots, and if made or missed, she continues to the next spot. Continue for one minute. Refer to Figure 2.4.

- Free throws (F.T.) – Player gets 10 shots.

- 3-pointers (3 Pt) – Player shoots three shots from designated spots. No time limit, but she will need a rebounder or a rack of balls next to her.

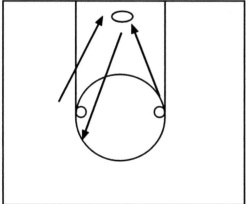

Figure 2.3. Lay-ups.

Figure 2.4. Hot-shot spots.

PASSING DRILL

- Long pass accuracy – Standing at the baseline, the player must use an overhand pass or baseball pass to opposite side of court, aiming for the cones (or players). Count number of close passes to target. She should make at least three attempts at each target. Refer to Figure 2.5.

DRIBBLING DRILLS

- Right hand speed dribble (R.H.) – Dribble the length of the court and back.

- Left hand speed dribble (L.H.) – Dribble the length of the court and back.

- Cone dribble – Dribble through cones the length of the floor and back.

- Zigzag dribble (ZZDr.) – Set up 10 cones as illustrated. The first person lines up at cone #1. At the whistle, she dribbles to cone #2, uses a crossover dribble, and heads to cone #3. The crossover dribble is used at every cone. Remind the players to keep their heads up while dribbling. Refer to Figure 2.6.

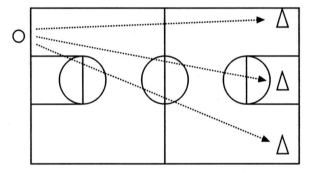

Figure 2.5. Long pass accuracy.

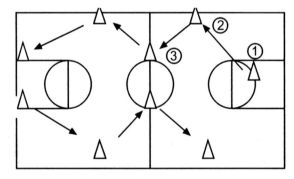

Figure 2.6. Zigzag dribble.

AGILITY DRILLS

- Lane slides – The athlete places her left foot on the lane and, on the whistle, she slides from line to line. The athlete should touch the line with her hand, never cross her feet, and stay as low as possible. Refer to Figure 2.7. A score may be assessed by either of two methods:

  ❑ Number of lines touched in 30 seconds

  ❑ The time it takes to touch 10 lines.

- Agility run – You can do a variety of things with an agility run. The following two options can get you started. Refer to Figure 2.8 and 2.9.
  - ❑ Shuttle run (Sht. Rn.)
  - ❑ Dummy run

EXPLOSION TEST

- Vertical jump (V.J.) – Put a strip of tape on the wall and label it in one-inch increments. Each player should stand flat-footed and reach up and touch the tape. Make a note of the measurement. She then gets one step to jump up and touch the tape. If you prefer, they can just stand and jump with no step, but it should be the same for everyone, of course. As she jumps and touches the tape, note the measurement. Subtract the first measurement from the second measurement to get her vertical jump distance. Give each player at least two attempts.

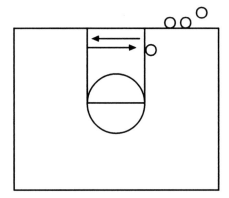

Figure 2.7. Lane slides.

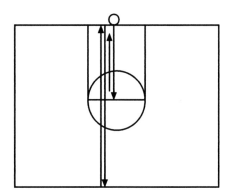

Figure 2.8. Shuttle run.

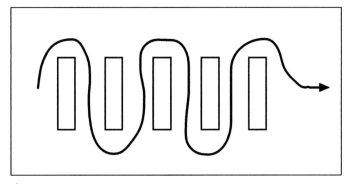

Figure 2.9. Dummy run.

ENDURANCE TEST

- Two-mile run or one-mile run (1-mile) – The two-mile run is the real endurance test, but because of time factors, a one-mile run will do. If you have a large group, run them in heats to make it easier to record their times. As each runner crosses the finish line, a coach should call out the time. Then have her walk ahead to another coach to record her time.

GAMES/SCRIMMAGES

Because this will be a subjective evaluation, put pairs and groups of players together whom you'd like to see play:

- 1-on-1 half-court games
- 3-on-3 half-court games
- 5-on-5 full-court scrimmage

SAMPLE EVALUATION FORM

You'll need a form to record times and attempts for your entire team. Since there are so many tests, you may choose not to use them all. Figure 2.10 illustrates an example of a form that can be employed in this regard. Each athlete should have her own evaluation form as well. Although this seems like a lot of paperwork, utilize your assistant coaches or managers to transfer information. Figure 2.11 shows a sample form that can be used by athletes.

CHOOSING THE TEAMS

After you have assessed everyone's skills and are ready to cut players, you usually end up having a hard time with some that are "on the fringe." You might bring those players back the next day and let those who have already made the team go home. This step will give the girls who are fighting for a position a clear idea of who they have to beat to be on the team.

As coaches, we know life is full of challenges and disappointments, but that's hard for most young women to understand. If you have to cut players, then bring each one in and talk to her personally, rather than posting a list. Show them their evaluation forms, and talk to them about how they can improve in the off-season.

2002-2003 Team Evaluations

Date: _____

Evaluation ___ of ___

Name	L.U.	Ht.Sht.	F.T.	3 Pt	R.H.	L.H.	ZZDr.	Sht. Rn.	V.J.	1-mile

Figure 2.10. Sample team evaluation form.

Name: Classification:

Event	Best Time/Attempt	Points Awarded
Lay-ups		
Hot-shot		
Free throws		
3-point shots		
Right-hand speed dribble		
Left-hand speed dribble		
Zigzag dribble		
Lane slides		
Shuttle run		
Vertical jump		
1-mile		
	TOTAL	

Subjective Evaluation:

1-on-1:

3-on-3:

5-on-5:

Leadership skills:

Work ethic:

Academic standing:

Attendance:

Figure 2.11. Sample player evaluation form.

ASSIGNING PLAYERS TO POSITIONS

Categorize your players according to a number using the following guidelines:

   #1: Point guard – runs offense, needs to be quick, and must handle the ball well

   #2: Off guard – helps handle the ball and is a shooting guard

   #3: Small forward – plays inside at low post or outside as a guard

   #4: Big forward (post) – inside player

   #5: Center (post) – inside player

   These categories define best-case scenarios. As a rule, you will generally play three guards and two post players on the court at a time.

CHOOSING YOUR GAME PLAN

Regardless of the level of play, there are many aspects to consider before the season. You could decide to be a very aggressive team that full-court presses the entire game and utilizes the fast-break or you could play a much slower, conservative style. If you have an inexperienced group, there is no way they can perfect every aspect of the game. As a result, you must decide what areas are most important and teach those things well.

   A list of some of the more appropriate aspects of the game that generally need to be taught at three different skill levels includes the following:

BEGINNER

As a general rule, the most popular group in this category will be junior high teams, although there may be some freshman or junior varsity teams that fall into this category as well. Make sure these players learn the following:

- Basic fundamentals (dribbling, passing, shooting, and rebounding)
- One or two zone defenses (2-3 or 1-3-1)
- Press breaks
- Two or three offensive plays vs. zone and man-to-man defenses
- Good transition
- Two inbounds plays
- A sideline play

INTERMEDIATE

Once a team has mastered the basic fundamentals of the game, the following aspects can be addressed:

- Zone press (2-2-1)
- More offensive plays and some "quick-hitters"
- Man-to-man defense with no switch on screens
- Fast-break

ADVANCED

The following areas from a teaching standpoint, are most appropriate for your varsity level athletes who are proficient in their basic fundamentals and understand the game fairly well:

- Aggressive zone press and man-to-man deny press
- Half-court trap
- Man-to-man defense with switch on screens
- Jump ball play
- Stall
- Quick transition game
- Last-second shot scenarios

A QUICK TEST TO GAUGE YOUR TEAM'S STRENGTHS AND WEAKNESSES

❑ Does your team have overall speed and quickness? If so, then full-court pressure and fast-break transition would work well.

❑ Do you have a great one-on-one player? If the answer is yes, then consider using some clear-out series and quick-hitters that allow her to utilize her skills.

❑ Is your team well-skilled in ballhandling and able to penetrate? If so, then patterned offenses would work well.

❑ Do you have good post players with superior height? If the answer is yes, then use double low-post or high-low post offenses and 1-4 offensive sets.

A CHECKLIST OF SKILLS

To be successful, you need to follow a master schedule so that all aspects of the game are covered. The following basic checklist is just something to get you started. You have to decide what is important for your team to accomplish before the first game and throughout the season.

- ❏ Basic fundamentals (dribbling, passing, shooting, and rebounding)
- ❏ Zone defenses
- ❏ Press breaks
- ❏ Offensive plays vs. zone and man-to-man
- ❏ Transition
- ❏ Inbounds plays
- ❏ Sideline plays
- ❏ "Quick-hitters"
- ❏ Man-to-man defense with and without switch on screens
- ❏ Fast-break
- ❏ Zone press
- ❏ Man-to-man deny press
- ❏ Half-court trap
- ❏ Jump ball play
- ❏ Stall
- ❏ Last-second shot plays

PUTTING IT ALL ON A TIMELINE

Break your season down into phases and determine what your teaching emphasis should be during each phase. Then, write down general areas you want to cover during the week so that nothing is left out. Once the season begins, you should refer to this master plan and use it to write detailed practice plans. You will have to make changes according to the development of your team, but having a solid master plan to work from will be helpful.

- Phase #1 (pre-season):
    - ❏ Cover your checklist of skills.
    - ❏ Develop a good conditioning base.
    - ❏ Improve individual offensive skills.
    - ❏ Improve individual defensive skills.

- Phase #2 (in-season):

    ❏ Note team weaknesses and plan practices to target them.

    ❏ Incorporate more offensive and defensive plays.

    ❏ Add quick-hitters, full-court presses, and half-court presses.

    ❏ Practice special situation drills daily.

- Phase #3 (off-season):

(A detailed plan of action is outlined in Chapter 11, *Off-Season Training*)

CHAPTER 3

Planning a Practice

The time your team spends practicing is valuable. Don't waste any of it. If you let your players drag into the gym, then you may have lost three minutes that day. Those three minutes a day over the course of a school year become nine hours of missed practice time. After planning for your season, you have the task of breaking it all down into individual workouts designed to target the needs of your team. Ensuring that your team's practice time is well-organized and well-spent requires that you address several areas, including a general practice outline, a master practice outline, a daily practice schedule, and other practice concerns.

GENERAL PRACTICE OUTLINE

Each practice should contain all of the following segments:

- Meetings
- Warm-up
- Individual skill work
- Team offense
- Team defense
- Game-situation drills
- Special situations
- Scrimmage
- Conditioning

❑ Meetings

Use the time set aside for meetings to:
- Address issues brought up in the leadership council meeting.
- Watch and critique film.
- Do some "chalk-talk" to explain a new offense, defense, drill, etc.
- Discuss a rule-of-the-day.

❑ Warm-up

The warm-up should start with some laps around the court to loosen the players' muscles. Stretch immediately following the running to help prevent any pulls or strains. Next, run a drill that involves all your players and is quick and fun. Conclude this component by getting the team together in a huddle and "break out" to go to the next drill.

❑ Individual skill work

During this period, you should have all players involved in a drill. Use stations around the court to ensure that no one is idle. (For rebounding, shooting, passing, and free throw drills, see Chapter 5.) The following seven-station set-up can be used to work on individual skill development (refer to Figure 3.1):

Station 1: Jump rope – two feet, left foot, right foot, double jumps

Station 2: Rebounding

Station 3: Taking a charge – work one-on-one (need a coach to supervise)

Station 4: Dribbling – right-handed, left-handed, speed dribble, crossover

Station 5: Shooting

Station 6: Passing

Station 7: Free-throw shooting

Allot a five-minute or 10-minute segment for each station. When the buzzer sounds, encourage the players to *hustle* to the next station.

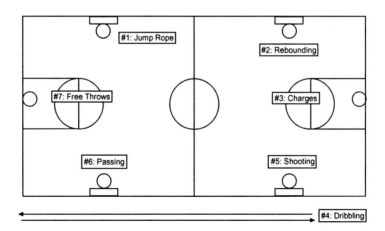

Figure 3.1. Sample station set-up.

❑ Team offense

Practice your offensive plays during this segment. Your substitutes should be as knowledgeable as your starters, so it is important that they get plenty of practice here as well. Have a first team, second team, third team, etc. and hustle them on and off the floor. Although some players will have idle time, keep the practice moving so they don't lose interest. Work your press breaks and inbounds plays in addition to your offensive plays.

❑ Team defense

Even though you will have a defensive scout team on the floor when practicing your offense, this is the time to focus on stopping your upcoming opponent. Your offensive scout team should run your next opponent's plays, giving the defense a purpose. Work your press (half-court, full-court, etc.) and defense of inbounds plays as well.

❑ Game-situation drills

These drills are designed to create game-like pressure during the team's practice time. Setting a goal and instituting consequences for failing to reach that goal is how this "pressure" is created. (Refer to the section on game-situation drills in Chapter 4.) Spend at least 20 minutes of practice on two or three of these drills.

❑ Special situations

This segment is a time to practice those situations that aren't common to every game but may be the difference between a win and a loss. The drills found in Chapter 4 give you the opportunity to create your own situations. For example, "ten seconds left, your team behind by three points, and you have the ball under the opponent's basket." Although the number of special situations is endless, spend at least ten minutes each day working on one particular situation.

❑ Scrimmage

Many days this will be an intersquad scrimmage. To increase the level of intensity and competition, scrimmage your varsity players against the junior varsity boys' team. Likewise, try junior varsity girls vs. freshmen boys; eighth grade girls vs. seventh grade boys; and seventh grade girls vs. eighth grade girls.

❑ Conditioning

The players will be getting quite a bit of conditioning by just going through practice but a team that is in shape will win those tough games in the fourth quarter. The conditioning could be contingent on free throw shooting. Two drills in Chapter 4 are great practice-ending drills (*three-in-a-row* and the *lucky shooter*).

MASTER PRACTICE OUTLINE

Write down all of your favorite drills for each component of practice and make a master practice outline. As a result, you won't have to hunt or browse through your drill books to find what drills you like.

Component	Drills
• Warm-up	10 laps in three minutes, 3-man weave, time-line drill, full-court tip drill, four corners, 3-on-2, 2-on-1, zigzag dribble, full speed lay-ups, star drill, weave drill, quick slides across lane
• Individual Skills Stations	*Use the set-up in the Individual Skill Work section of this chapter.*
• Shooting	Individual shooting, two-man drill, stamina drill, two-line lay-ups, in-and-out shooting, six-hoop shooting, five-spot conditioning, full-court frenzy, knock out, rebound-speed, shooting for the record
• Passing	Keep away, simple shuttle drill, four corners, star drill
• Rebounding	Blind box out, circle box out, three-and-out
• Dribbling	Weave drill, tag, zigzag dribble
• Team Offense	Your offensive plays, press breaks, in-bounds plays, quick-hitters
• Team Defense	Your defensive systems, presses, in-bounds defense
• Game Situations	Choose two or three each practice.
• Special Situations	Choose one or two each practice.
• Scrimmage	Play against other squads, if possible.
• Conditioning	Sprints, suicides, horses, etc., or free throw drills – three-in-a-row or the lucky shooter

THE DAILY PRACTICE SCHEDULE

A common practice among football coaches is to break a practice down into segments. Each segment represents five minutes of practice time. A similar method can be used by women's basketball coaches.

Have a manager sit at the clock and hit the horn at the end of each five-minute segment and keep track using the numbers on the scoreboard. A sample schedule form is illustrated in Figure 3.2. When using the sample schedule shell, write the drills you'd like to use under each heading to keep yourself organized.

OTHER PRACTICE CONCERNS

❏ First game preparation

As you prepare for your first game, explain to your less experienced players the procedures for subbing in a game, time-outs, free throw rules and procedures, and jump ball rules and procedures. Practice these things during scrimmages and then have an intersquad scrimmage with officials, a game clock, and a scorekeeper. This step will help eliminate any confusion on game day.

Time	Period	Activity
2:30	1	Warm-up
	2	
2:40	3	Individual skills
	4	
	5	
	6	
3:00	7	Team offense
	8	
	9	
	10	
3:20	11	Team defense
	12	
	13	
	14	
3:40	15	Break
3:45	16	Game situations
	17	
3:55	18	Special situations
	19	
4:05	20	Scrimmage
	21	
	22	
4:20	23	Conditioning
	24	
4:30	25	End practice

Figure 3.2. Sample practice schedule form.

❑ Communication

Teach communication skills as well. The team should communicate switches on screens, back-door cutters, dead ball, and other situations. During free throws, your point guard should check in with you so she knows exactly what you want. She can do this by coming to the sideline on a two-shot foul. If you choose to signal plays from the bench, then you should practice these as well in scrimmage situations. A signal to stall, press, change the defense, or call an offense would be effective in helping to throw off the opposing team.

❑ Practicing during the holidays

Depending on the situation, most junior high teams normally get the Thanksgiving and Christmas breaks off, but practicing during these times can be optional. If you have the gym open for practice, most of the team will probably come. High school teams, on the other hand, rarely have a very long break over the holidays. In fact, most high school teams play games or participate in tournaments during these breaks. As a result, practicing is crucial during these times, especially when players are tempted with "lots of goodies to eat." Practicing during the holidays enables you to avoid losing in a matter of two weeks what you've practiced so hard for up to that point.

CHAPTER 4

Drills

The number and variety of drills available to basketball coaches is too numerous to list. As a result, this chapter includes selected drills for improving each skill, along with a few of my favorites.

BALLHANDLING DRILLS

❑ **Around the body:**

- Pass the ball around your stomach as quickly as possible – reverse after one minute.
- Put your legs together, pass the ball around your legs, then reverse.
- Split your legs and circle around your left leg.
- Circle around your right leg.
- Perform a figure eight through both legs.

❑ **Single leg circle:**

- Dribble the ball around your right leg.
- Dribble the ball around your left leg.
- Put your feet together and dribble around both legs.

❏ **Wall dribble:**

- Dribble the ball against the wall above your head.
- Control the ball with your fingertips.
- Dribble for 30 seconds.
- Switch to your left hand and repeat.

❏ **Figure eight drills:**

- Dribble the ball around your right leg.
- Switch the ball into your left hand and dribble around your left leg.
- Bring the ball around back between your legs and continue.

❏ **Hand switch:**

- Place the ball between your legs, holding it with your right arm in front and left arm in back.
- Allow the ball to bounce once as you switch your hand position.
- As your quickness improves, do not let the ball drop.

❏ **Butterfly dribble:**

- Place the ball on the floor between your legs.
- Tap the ball with your right hand, followed by a tap with your left hand.
- With your right hand behind one leg, tap again with both hands.
- Keep the ball between your legs during a continuous dribble.

INDIVIDUAL SHOOTING DRILLS

❏ **Guards** (all moves done ten times with right hand, then with left hand):

- Shot fake – dribble right – shoot
- Shot fake – dribble right – crossover – shoot
- Shot fake – dribble right – between legs dribble – shoot
- Shot fake – dribble right – behind back dribble – shoot

- Shot fake – dribble right – spin move – one dribble – shoot
- Standing set shots from six positions on court (20 shots at each)
- Free throws (at least 50 per workout)

❑ **Post players** (move to left block after all moves done ten times)

- On right block, simulate pass – drop step (left foot) with one dribble – shoot
- On right block, simulate pass – fake left – turn around jump shot
- On right block, simulate pass – fake right – drop step – shoot
- Continuous baby jump shots from each block

SMALL-GROUP SHOOTING DRILLS

The key for the illustrations used to clarify the drills included in this chapter is presented in Figure 4.1.

❑ **Two-spot shooting** (Refer to Figure 4.2)

Set-Up: One ball, two players

Directions: Player 1 starts at one elbow and shoots, while player 2 rebounds. After the shot, player 1 moves to the other elbow, immediately receives a pass from player 2, and shoots. This pattern continues for one minute, and then the players switch.

❑ **Stamina drill** (Refer to Figure 4.3)

Set-Up: Two balls, three players

Directions: Player 1 has a ball ready to shoot, player 3 has a ball under the basket, and player 2 is on the court. Player 1 shoots and gets her own

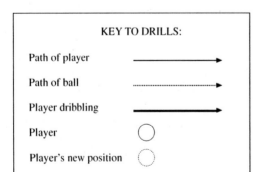

Figure 4.1. Drill key.

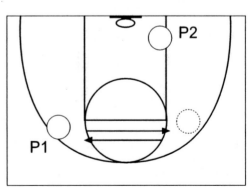

Figure 4.2. Two-spot shooting drill.

rebound. Player 3 passes the ball to player 2 and pops out, ready for a pass from player 1. Player 2 gets her own rebound and passes to player 1. The cycle continues for about one minute.

❑ **In-and-out shooting** (Refer to Figure 4.4)

Set-Up: Two lines facing the basket with two players in the lane to receive a pass. Line #1 works the drill just like line#2.

Directions: Player 1 passes to the teammate directly in front of her in the lane (player 2), then sprints out to receive a return pass. Player 1 shoots, and player 2 rebounds, and then passes to player 3. Players switch lines after each shot, while rebounders in the paint rotate after ten passes.

❑ **Full-court frenzy** (Refer to Figure 4.5)

Set-Up: Two players, each with a ball, line up on different ends of the court facing each other.

Directions: Players sprint to the opposite basket and shoot only once. After one shot is taken, the players rebound and return to the other end of the court. Again, one shot is taken and scored accordingly. The next player in line gets the rebound and sprints to the opposite goal. This procedure continues for either a certain time period or until the entire team shoots.The players get points based on where the shot was taken on the floor:

Three-point line = four pts   In the paint =   two pts
Free throw line = three pts   Lay-up = one pt

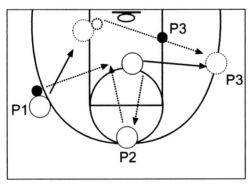

Figure 4.3. Stamina drill.

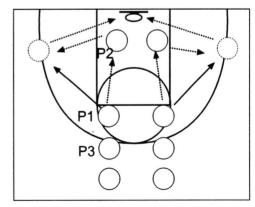

Figure 4.4. In-and-out shooting drill.

❏ **Three-man weave** (Refer to Figure 4.6)

Set-Up: Start with three lines under a basket, with the ball in the middle line.

Directions: The middle player begins by throwing the ball to her right and following her pass behind the teammate who received it. The player with the ball then throws to the teammate on her left and follows her pass. This procedure continues down the floor until one player is close enough to shoot a lay-up and continue back down the floor.

❏ **3-on-2, 2-on-1** (Refer to Figure 4.7)

Set-Up: Three players set up like the start of the 3-man weave with two players on defense at the other end.

Directions: The three players go down the floor and attempt to score. When the defense gets the ball, the player who shoots the ball now has to run back and play defense against the two who were playing defense against the 3-on-2. The other two members of the 3-on-2 team who didn't shoot are now on defense, waiting for the next group of three to come down.

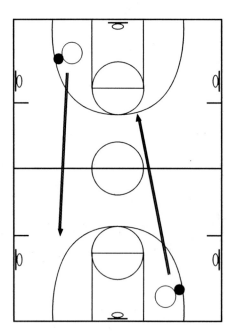

Figure 4.5. Full-court frenzy drill.

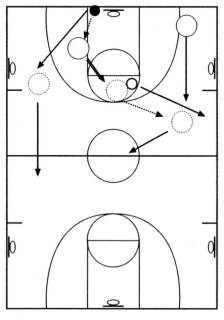

Figure 4.6. Three-man weave drill.

❑ **Timeline drill** (Refer to Figure 4.8)

Set-Up: Begin with a line of players at each hashmark (or timeline). One player stands under each basket with a ball (player 1).

Directions: Player 1 passes to player 2, who immediately passes it back to player 1. She then passes to player 3 (while sprinting down the floor) and again receives it back. She then goes in for a lay-up. Player 1 moves to line 2; player 2 moves to line 3; and player 3 follows player 1 and gets the rebound. At this point, the rebounder continues down the opposite side of the floor as player 1. See how many baskets can be made in a row for a certain time limit and work them clockwise and counterclockwise.

❑ **Full-court tip drill** (Refer to Figure 4.9)

Set-Up: Line up half of your players facing one basket and the other half facing the opposite basket. Each line has one ball.

Directions: The first player in each line tosses the ball up softly off of the backboard. The second player in line jumps up and tips it against the board, followed by the third player, and so on. After tipping the ball, each player must sprint to the opposite basket and get in line until it is her turn to tip on that end Each time the ball hits the floor, the players accumulate one sprint to be run at the end of the drill. The objective is to go for an entire minute without stopping.

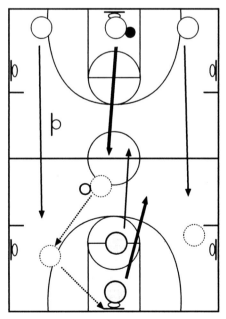

Figure 4.7. 3-on-2, 2-on-1 drill.

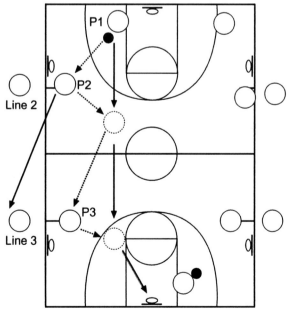

Figure 4.8. Timeline drill.

Variation: You can lower the time for younger players and allow a few to hit the floor before the accumulation of sprints. For older players, set a limit to the number of times the ball is allowed to hit the floor and once that limit is reached, stop the drill, run, and start over.

❑ **Full speed lay-ups** (Refer to Figure 4.10)

Set-Up: Divide the team with half on each end of the court. Have a coach stand on the elbow at one end and another coach stand on the elbow at the other end. On both ends of the court, have a player step out with a ball.

Directions: The first player tosses the ball up against the backboard, rebounds it, and passes to the coach on the elbow. The player then takes off and receives a pass from the coach. Both players shoot a lay-up, while next player in line waits to rebound the ball. She passes the ball back to the coach and then gets a return pass. She then shoots a lay-up. Run the drill for two to three minutes and set a goal for number of baskets made.

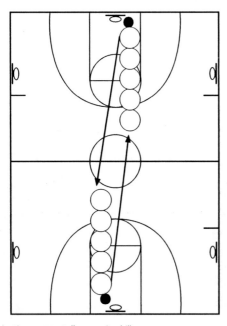

Figure 4.9. Full-court tip drill.

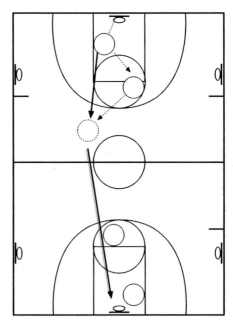

Figure 4.10. Full-speed lay-up drill.

❑ Knock out

Set-Up: The team lines up at the foul line. The first two players each have a ball.

Directions: The first player shoots and once the ball is released, the second player shoots. If the player who is behind makes her shot before the front player, then the front player is knocked out of the game and has to sit out. If the front player makes her shot and the second player has not, she is still in the game. She passes the ball to the next player in line who is now the back player and is trying to knock out the second shooter who is now the front player. The first shot comes from the foul line, but other shots can come from anywhere (lay-ups too). If a player does not get knocked out, she goes to the back of the line. The winner is the last player standing.

Variations: All shots have to be outside the paint, or the first shot begins at the three-point line.

SHOOTING FOR THE RECORD

Using any of the drills in this section, record total baskets made in a pre-determined time period or consecutive baskets made. Encourage your players to try to improve on their performance in the drills each time and keep track of their performance the entire season.

FREE-THROW SHOOTING DRILLS

❑ Three-in-a-row

Set-Up: Three players are positioned at the free-throw line, while the rest of team stands on the baseline.

Directions: Three players go to the free-throw line to shoot one shot at a time. If all three shots are made, the next three players come up to shoot free throws—one at a time. If any shots are missed, the whole team will run a sprint (baseline to baseline within 13 seconds). After the sprints are completed, the next three players come out to shoot. Any missed shots will cause the entire team to run. Every player must make a free throw before going on to the next drill or ending practice.

❑ The lucky shooter

Set-Up: One shooter is at the free-throw line, while rest of team stands on the baseline.

Directions: The shooter has two shots. If she makes both, the team doesn't run. If she misses one, the whole team does a full-court sprint. If she misses both, the whole team runs a suicide (free-throw line and back; half-court line and back; etc.). You could conduct the drill once as stated, or if the player misses both, have her shoot again with the same punishment.

❑ **Climbing the ladder** (Refer to Figure 4.11):

• Using a bulletin board or some plywood that's visible in the gym, put pins or nails down the length of the board about two to three inches apart. Make sure you have a spot for each player.

• Using round, metal-rimmed tags, put each player's name on one and hang each of them at random.

• Each player on the board pairs up with her opponent who is the player directly above them and shoots 10 - 50 free throws.

• Whoever makes the most moves up, while the loser moves down.

• The only way to advance is to beat a player that's above you.

• The player in the top spot competes every other day to allow players in the #3 and below spots to move up.

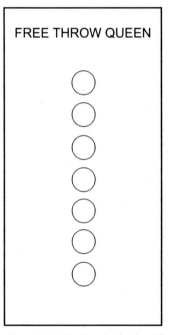

Figure 4.11. Climbing the ladder drill.

PASSING AND CATCHING DRILLS

A checklist of passes to teach:

❑ Two-handed chest pass   ❑ Bounce pass

❑ One-handed push pass   ❑ Two-handed overhead pass

❑ Baseball pass   ❑ Lob pass

❑ **Keep away drill**

Set-Up: Offense set up to run at half-court, executing a man-to-man offense against defense

Directions: Offensive players may not shoot or dribble. The goal is to teach your players to get open by making good cuts or setting screens. Any time the defense touches the ball or steals a pass it counts against the offense. Run the drill for a minute or two and allow for a certain number of touches or steals by the defense. If that limit is reached before time expires, stop the drill, run the players, and start the drill again.

❑ **Simple shuttle drill** (Refer to Figure 4.12)

Set-Up: Two lines facing each other

Directions: The first player in one line makes a chest pass to the first player in the other line, follows the pass, and gets in the back of the line. This continues until all have gone through at least once or twice. Change types of passes as soon as the player who started is at the front of the line again.

❑ **Four corners** (Refer to Figure 4.13)

Set-Up: Four players in the four corners

Directions: The drill starts with player 1 dribbling to make a lay-up from the right side, while player 2 rebounds the ball (P1 goes to P2's spot). Player 2, who has retrieved the ball, passes to player 3 on the outlet on the left side (P2 takes her place in line). Player 4 runs toward the center of the court and catches the pass from player 3. Player 3 goes to player 4's line. Player 4 passes to player 1 who is sprinting to shoot a lay-up. Player 4 then becomes player 1, and the drill starts over.

Variation: Add another ball into play.

❑ **Star drill** (Refer to Figure 4.14)

Set-Up: One line under the basket is needed with four players on the court:

- Player 1 – under basket
- Player 2 – left side of elbow
- Player 3 – right side block
- Player 4 – left side block
- Player 5 – right side of elbow

Directions: Player 1 starts the drill by passing to player 2. Player 1 replaces player 2. Player 2 passes to player 3 and replaces her. Player 3 passes to player 4 and replaces her. Player 4 passes to player 5, who shoots a lay-up. Player 6 rebounds and begins the cycle again.

Variations: Change directions so players shoot a left-handed lay-up and/or have each player sprint to the corner of the half-court area before receiving the next pass.

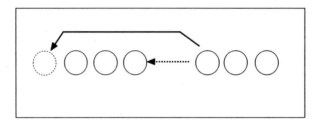

Figure 4.12. Simple shuttle drill.

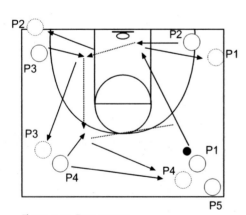

Figure 4.13. Four corners.

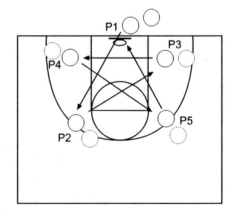

Figure 4.14. Star drill.

REBOUNDING AND BLOCKING OUT DRILLS

❑ Blind block out

Set-Up: Start with three players standing outside the three-point line and three other players laying face down in the lane with their eyes covered.

Directions: One of the players shoots the ball and yells "Shot!" When the players in the paint hear this, they must get up and find a man to block out. The defense must get five rebounds before the offense gets three rebounds.

❑ Circle box out

Set-Up: Place a basketball on the floor in the center of the half-court circle or a free-throw-line circle. Two pairs of players start at each circle.

Directions: On the whistle, the inside player attempts to keep her partner from getting the ball by blocking her out. After 10 to 15 seconds, blow the whistle again and have the players switch positions.

DRIBBLING DRILLS

❑ Weave drill

Set-Up: Players line up single file along the sideline with one ball in front and one in back.

Directions: As the players jog around the outside of the court, the ball in front is passed back over the heads of the players, and the ball at the back is dribbled forward through the line, weaving through the players. Each time the ball reaches the front, it is passed back overhead. Each time the ball reaches the back of the line, it is dribbled through the line to the front. Run the drill for a certain number of laps or for a predetermined time limit.

❑ Tag (Refer to Figure 4.15)

Set-Up: Position the whole team in the area between both free-throw lines and the sidelines. Give each player a ball, depending upon number available.

Directions: The players dribble, staying out of the boundaries, while trying to knock the ball away from the other players. If a player loses her dribble, stops her dribble, or goes out of the boundaries, she leaves the game. When the number of players gets down to five or six, change the boundary to the center circle.

❏ **Zigzag dribble** (Refer to Figure 4.16)

Set-Up: Set up 10 cones as illustrated in Figure 4.16. The players line up at
               cone #1.

Directions: Player 1 dribbles to cone #2, uses a crossover dribble, and heads to
               cone #3. The crossover dribble is used at every cone. When player 1
               is at cone #2, the next player in line starts the drill. Remind the players
               to keep their heads up while dribbling.

Variations: The players pivot at each cone or cross over behind their back.

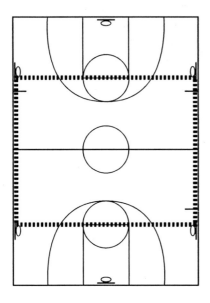

Figure 4.15. Tag.

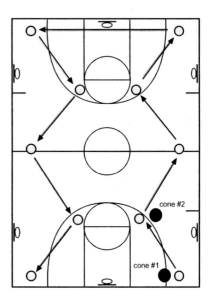

Figure 4.16. Zigzag dribble.

INDIVIDUAL DEFENSE AND CONDITIONING DRILLS

❏ **Quick slides across the lane** (Refer to Figure 4.17)

Set-Up: Line up players on one sideline in four lines.

Directions: The first players in each line stand with their left foot positioned on the
               edge of the paint, facing the coach. On the coach's command, those
               players slide, using a good defensive stance, back and forth across the
               lane, touching each line with their hand. After about five trips across
               the lane, they turn and sprint to the opposite sideline. The next four
               players sprint to the lane and begin again. Once everyone has gone
               through the drill, it is repeated from the right-hand side. Emphasize
               good form, staying low, and not crossing the legs.

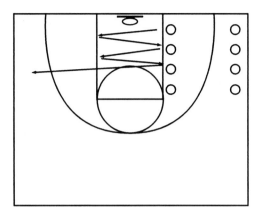

Figure 4.17. Quick slides across the lane.

❏ Sprints, suicides, horses, etc.

Set-Up: The entire team starts at the baseline.

Directions: The team must do any of the following:

- Sprint the length of the floor and back – five times in 51 seconds.

- Run to the free-throw line, back; half-court, back; next free-throw line, back; opposite baseline, back – one time in 35 seconds.

- Sprint to the half-court, back; full-court, back – one time in 13 seconds.

- Sprint forward to the opposite baseline; backpedal to the starting point. On the last trip, make the finish line at the free-throw line to keep players from running into the wall – four times in 55 seconds.

❏ 16 Candles

Set-Up: Line up the players on the sideline.

Directions: Run sideline to sideline – 16 times in one minute.

GAME SITUATION DRILLS

❏ Drill #1

Set-Up: The starting five on offense is on the court; all others off the court. No defense.

Directions: The offense, running a half-court offense, must score five times before missing three shots. Rotate teams after "defense" scores three misses or home scores 10 points.

Variations: Add five defensive players and award points for steals and misses.

❏ **Drill #2**

Set-Up: Two mixed teams with starters on both (#1, #2, #3 on offense and #4, #5 on defense). The scout team fills in the rest. Play five-on-five.

Directions: The defense starts at 10 points. The offense runs a half-court offense. A turnover by the offense or a steal by the defense is one point for the defense. Offense scores two points for each basket. Play to 20.

❏ **Drill #3**

Set-Up: Two mixed teams with starters on both. Play five-on-five.

Directions: Coach shoots ball. Whether made or missed, the defense runs a fast break and must score. Must score five times before missing three.

Variations: Give the offense 10 points and require the defense to get 20 to beat them; put one or two players under the opposite basket before they run the fast break. Total of six or seven on defense.

❏ **Drill #4**

Set-Up: Two full teams.

Directions: The coach shoots, and if basket is made, the offense must press. The offense should be down by five to ten points and score on steals.

❏ **Drill #5**

Set-Up: Six defensive players and five on offense.

Directions: The defense plays man-to-man, while one extra defensive player stays in the lane. The offense must score 10 points before the defense steals the ball three times.

❏ **Drill #6**

Set-Up: Two full teams.

Directions: The offense must make six quick passes before scoring. The offense must make passes and score to earn points. The defense starts with 10 points. The game ends when one team reaches 20 points.

❏ **Drill #7**

Set-Up: Two mixed teams with starters on both.

Directions: Full-court scrimmage. Give the opposing team one point for steals in addition to points scored by made baskets.

❏ **Drill #8**

Set-Up: Two full teams set up for a free throw.

Directions: The shooting team must secure the rebound and score.

Variation: Give the defense five points and require the shooting team to reach 10 points to beat them.

❏ **Drill #9**

Set-Up: Starting five on offense running an in-bounds play.

Directions: The offense must score on in-bounds play immediately. If the defense steals the ball or if the ball is turned over, the defense gets a point. The offense scores one point for a made basket. Play to 10.

❏ **Drill #10**

Set-Up: Starting five on defense against in-bounds play.

Directions: The defense must hold the offense to five-second penalty or steal the ball to get a point. The offense scores by getting the ball in-bounds successfully. Play to 10.

❏ **Drill #11**

Set-Up: Starting five on a press break with six to eight defensive players pressing.

Directions: The offense must work the ball through without a turnover. The offense scores if it is successful at getting the ball across half-court. The defense gets points on steals, turnovers, and holding the offense to 10 seconds. The offense must be successful five times before defense scores three points.

❏ **Drill #12**

Set-Up: Starting five or mixed group with starters on both teams.

Directions: The offense must successfully run one minute off the clock while in stall before the defense gets the ball or the ball is turned over.

Variation: Add additional defensive players and/or increase the amount of time the offense is required to run off the clock.

❑ Drill #13

Set-Up: Two full teams at half-court.

Directions: The game is played to 10. The *offense* starts with the ball and gets points for the following:

- one point – made basket
- two points – lay-up
- three points – rebound

The *defense* gets points for the following:

- one point – rebound
- two points – steal or offensive turnover
- three points – taking a charge

Variations: Use several teams of five and rotate, leaving losers on the court. Change point totals to emphasize a different aspect of the game (e.g. five points for steals or four points for rebounds).

❑ Drill #14

Set-Up: Four groups of three players.

Directions: The teams play full court. When a team scores, the defense immediately inbounds the ball and heads down court on offense. The first team to score three to five baskets wins and leaves the court. The losers stay.

SPECIAL SITUATION DRILLS

This section is designed to allow you to create your own drills by changing four key components: time/points, score, possession, and position of the ball. These last-second scenarios are most effective if practiced daily and practiced against another team. For example, seventh-grade girls vs. eighth-grade girls; eighth-grade girls vs. seventh-grade boys; junior-varsity girls vs. freshmen boys; and varsity girls vs. junior-varsity boys.

❑ Component #1: Time/point range constraints

Since it would be difficult to score more than 10 points in a 55-second period, the range for that time period is from one to 10 points. Likewise, because four points is probably the maximum you could score in 10 seconds, and three points in four seconds, the following scale is appropriate:

- 55 seconds = 1 to 10 points
- 10 seconds = 1 to 4 points
- 4 seconds = 1 to 3 points

❑ **Component #2: Score status**

In a game situation, you only have to deal with three situations: you are ahead, you are behind, or you are tied.

❑ **Component #3: Possession**

This, too, is fairly easy to determine. Either you have the ball or your opponents have it.

❑ **Component #4: Position**

This component determines how play begins, either by an inbounds play or shooting a free throw. This component can further be broken down by the area on the floor from which the ball is coming in and whether the free throw is a one-on-one situation or a two-shot foul. As a result, the following six variables exist:

- From the sideline – opponent's half of the court
- From the sideline – your half of the court
- Under your basket
- Under the opponent's basket
- Shooting a one-and-one free throw
- Shooting two free throws

Summary

This information has been compiled in a chart so you can pick and choose what you want. Choose one item from each category for each special situation drill. Use the chart illustrated in Figure 4.18.

TIME/PT RANGE	SCORE	POSSESSION	POSITION
• 55 sec (1-10 pts)	• behind	• your ball	• on the sideline
• 10 sec (1-4 pts)	• tied	• opponent's ball	• under your basket • under opponent's basket
• 4 sec (1-3 pts)	• ahead		• shooting one-and-one • shooting two

Figure 4.18.

Examples of special situation drills:

- 10 seconds left – your team is behind by three points. You have the ball under the opponent's basket.
- 55 seconds left – the score is tied. Your opponents have the ball shooting a one-and-one.
- Four seconds left – your team is ahead by one. Your opponents have the ball under their basket.

As you can see, quite a few possibilities exist. Choose at least two of these drills for each practice.

❑ All-in-one drill

This drill is designed to cover as many aspects of the game as possible and should be used at least the day before the game. The idea is to prepare the team for as many different game situations as you can.

Set-Up: Use your first team and a scout team. Determine which baskets to defend as if it was a regular game. Each team is positioned on their own bench.

Directions: This drill is run at a walk-through speed, rather than real game-time speed. Work down the following list once with your starters and a second time with substitutes:

- Jump ball play – the first team scores
- Drop back in a 2-3 zone defense
- Scout team runs the offense – score
- Fast break offense – score
- Full-court press (whatever you choose: zone or man-to-man)
- Steal – score
- Drop back in a 1-3-1 zone defense
- Scout team shoots and misses
- Rebound
- Scout team in a man-to-man defense
- Run half-court offense (your choice)
- Shoot and miss – the scout team rebounds

- Sprint back and get in 2-3 zone defense
- Foul on the first team; the scout team shoots two
- Call time-out
- Sideline play – forced into half-court offense
- Run your half-court offense (the scout team in zone)
- Knocked out-of-bounds; retain possession under the basket
- Fouled – the first team shoots one-and-one
- Both shots made – no press; employ man-to-man defense
- Ball knocked out-of-bounds–the scout team's ball under their basket

CHAPTER 5

Team Offense

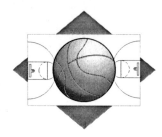

Regardless of the offense you choose, it will only be successful if you have athletes who can remember where to go and have mastered the basic fundamentals of shooting, dribbling, and passing. With a beginner-level team, actually running a play may be a tremendous accomplishment. This chapter will give you some basic plays vs. zone, man-to-man, and plays vs. specialty defenses such as the box-1 and the triangle-2.

OFFENSES VS. ZONE

Each of these plays can be repeated by reversing the ball until a high-percentage shot is available. Consider naming each offense to make it easy for your players to remember.

❑ **#1 — 2-3 alignment** (Refer to Figure 5.1)

❑ **#2 — 1-2-2 alignment** (Refer to Figure 5.2)

❑ **#3 — 1-2-2 alignment** (Refer to Figure 5.3)

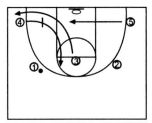

1 has the ball. 4 screens for 3 and the pops up to the elbow. 5 flashes to the low post on the ballside.

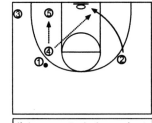

If 1 passes to 4, 4 can shoot, look for 5 down low, or pass to 2 cutting to basket.

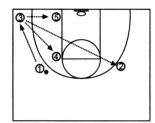

If 1 passes to 3 in corner, 3 can shoot, pass to 5 down low, or to 4 at high post who then can use options in previous set or skip pass to 2.

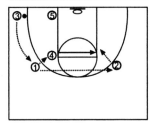

If 3 passes back to 1, 1 can pass to 4 if free or start a reversal by passing to 2 who looks to shoot or passes to 4 sliding across foul line.

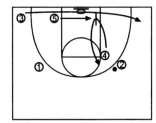

3 comes across end line to the opposite corner using a screen from 4; 4 then comes up the lane. 5 flashes to low-post ball side.

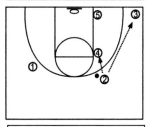

At this point, 2 has the same options as 1 at the beginning of the offense. Keep swinging the ball until a good shot is available.

Figure 5.1.

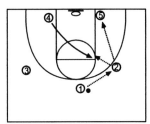

1 passes to 2, 4 flashes to high post, 2 looks to shoot or pass to 5. Next option is to look for 4.

If 4 gets the ball, she squares to shoot, passes inside to 5 or passes to the weakside to 3.

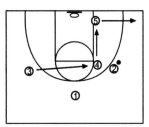

If 2 can't hit 4 or 5, then 5 pops out to wing, 4 drops to low post and 3 flashes to ball side elbow.

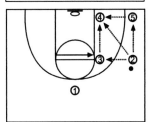

2 can shoot, pass to 3 flashing to elbow or pass inside to 4 or 5 in the corner. If 5 has ball, he can shoot, go to 4 or 3 or back to 2. If 3 gets the ball, shoots or passes to 2, 4, or 5.

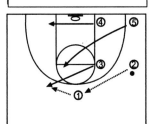

To reverse, ball goes from 2 to 1. 3 goes to original wing position. 1 passes to 3 while 4 flashes to low post and 5 goes to elbow on ball side.

3 looks for 4 or 5. If not open, 4 pops out to wing, 5 drops to low post, and 2 flashes to elbow on ball side. You're back in overload.

Figure 5.2.

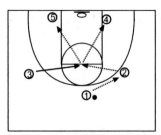

|  |  |

1 passes to 2 and 3 cuts to high post. If 3 receives pass, she looks for 4 or 5.	If 2 can't pass to 3, then she passes back to 1 and sets a screen with 4 or 3.	3 uses screen and pops out on wing. If 3 is not open, then 2 cuts over to opposite wing using screen set by 5. New sequence ready.

Figure 5.3.

ATTACKING THE BOX-1 AND TRIANGLE-2

The box-1 and triangle-2 are defenses you might not see too often but you must be prepared to attack them. You can do one of two things against these types of defenses: work to get your player(s) open who are being manned, or use an "overload-away" principle where you take your manned player(s) completely out of the play and overload one side of the zone.

❏ **#4 — 2-1-2 alignment** (Refer to Figure 5.4)

☆ =manned player

|  | 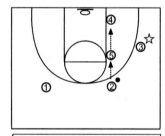 |

3 goes down to lane and pops out to wing getting screen from 4. 3 gets the ball and shoots if open.	If 3 is not open, she looks for 4 at low post, 5 flashing highpost, or 2 for reversal.	When 3 passes to 2, 2 looks for 5 at high post. If 5 gets ball, she squares to shoot or looks to 4.

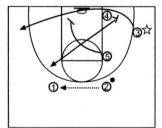

| 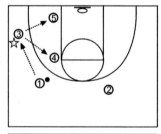 |  |

3 runs to baseline to opposite wing as soon as she sees reversal. 4 and 5 both set screens for 3. 1 looks to pass to 4 flashing up after screening for 3.	If 1 passes to 3 in the corner, then she has same options as left side.	If ball is reversed again, 3 can pop up to the middle of the lane instead of running baseline for a different look.

Figure 5.4.

#5 — "Overload-away" variation of Attacking Box-1 and Triangle-2 (Refer to Figure 5.5)

OFFENSES VS. MAN-TO-MAN

To effectively run a man-to-man offense your players must have good one-on-one skills, the ability to screen, and the ability to recognize scoring opportunities. There are generally two types of man offenses: set-patterned offenses and rule-oriented offenses. I will present two of each. A set-patterned offense would be more ideal for younger teams since a pattern is repeated until a high percentage shot comes available.

□ **#6 — 1-2-2 alignment** (Refer to Figure 5.6)

Box-1 Variation	Tri-2 Variation, #1	Tri-2 Variation, #2
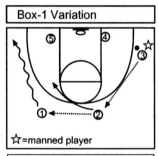		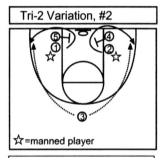
☆=manned player	☆=manned player	☆=manned player
As 3 passes back to 2 for reversal, she stays in corner and doesn't go to baseline. 2 passes to 1 and 1 dribbles into the corner. 2 replaces 1 creating a 3 on 2 vs. the defense.	1 and 2 set up in corners while 3 and 4 pass to each other. When 4 penetrates she either scores or draws defender away from 5 and passes to 5.	Set up in stack. 1 and 2 go down and around screens and pop out to corners for a pass from 3.

Figure 5.5.

	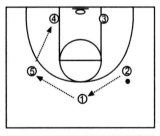	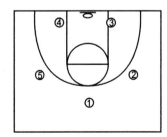
1 passes to 2. 3 cuts towards low post to set a screen for 4. As 3 cuts down, 2 looks to pass to 3 or waits for 4 flashing up the lane. As 3 goes to screen, 5 pops up and takes her place.	2 reverses ball to 1, who looks for 4. If not there, 1 passes to 5, who waits for 4 to drop to low post.	If 4 doesn't receive pass, then the pattern is repeated according to which wing receives first pass.

Figure 5.6.

❑ **#7 — 2-1-2 alignment** (Refer to Figure 5.7)

❑ **#8 — "Pass and screen away" — 1-2-2 alignment** (Refer to Figure 5.8)

Rule:　　*Pass and screen away*

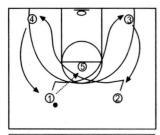

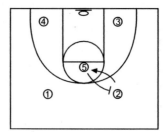

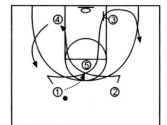

1 passes to 5 then cuts post, looking for a hand-off. 2 follows on the opposite side. 5 has the option of handing off, turning to shoot, or waiting for 2 to cut down. 4 and 5 pop up and replace 1 and 2.	If 5 isn't open, then 5 screens for 2 to start offense.	Variation: 1 passes to 5, 2 follows, but 3 sets screen for 1, who waits for ball. If not there, she pops to wing.

Figure 5.7.

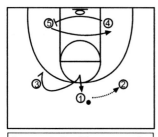

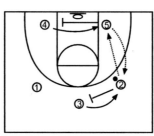

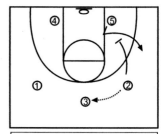

1 passes to 2 and then screens for 3. 4 waits briefly for a pass from 2 and then screens for 5.	If 2 passes to 5, she then screens for 3. If 5 passes out to 3, she screens for 4.	If 2 passes to 3, then she screens down for 5.

Figure 5.8.

❑ **#9 — "Flex"— 2-3 alignment** (Refer to Figure 5.9)

Rules:　　• *You make a pass, you set a screen.*

　　　　　　• *You set a screen, you get a screen.*

　　　　　　• *You get a screen, you catch a pass or set a screen*

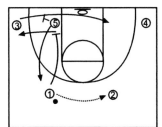

As 1 passes to 2, 5 turns and sets a pick for 3. Since 1 made a pass, she sets a pick for 5 and pops out to wing. 5 replaces 1 and 3 goes to opposite block.

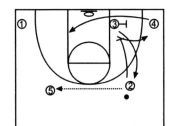

2 passes to 5 and 2 sets a pick for 3. 4 waits for the pass to 5 and gets a pick from 3. 3 replaces 2, 2 pops out to wing, and 4 goes to opposite block.

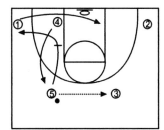

1 will wait for ball to go to 3 and will get a pick from 4, then go to opposite block. 4 will set a pick, wait for pick, and go high for a pass. 3 will wait for pass, then pass back to 4 and set a pick. 2 will wait for pass to 4 and go to opposite block.

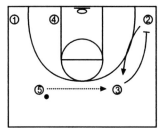

If 3 isn't open, 3 down-screens for 2.

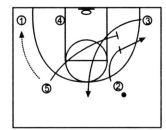

If 5 can't make the pass to 2, then 5 passes to 1 and sets a double pick with 2 for 3. 2 pops to the corner to replace 3. 3 goes to opposite side to get pass from 1. 5 comes back high to reset offense.

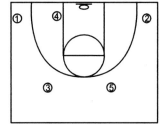

Once the offense is reset, you are back to the normal flex formation.

Figure 5.9.

CHAPTER 6

Special Plays

INBOUNDS PLAYS

Traditionally, two basic plays can be run under a goal: the box and the stack. From these two formations, you can be as creative as you want to be. When practicing inbounds plays, you should include at least one sideline play that can also be modified according to the strengths of your team.

- Box #1 (Refer to Figure 6.1)

- Box #2 (Refer to Figure 6.2)

- Box #3 (Refer to Figure 6.3)

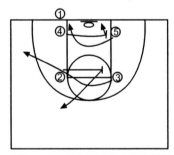

2 and 4 screen across the lane for 3 and 5. 4 turns immediately to the passer by pinning her girl behind her. 5 comes across lane looking for a pass. 3 cuts towards passer, and 2 pops out to top of key.

Figure 6.1.

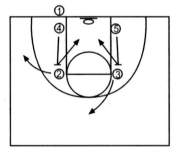

4 and 5 screen up for 2 and 3 and come back down the lane looking for ball. 2 pops out to wing, and 3 pops out to top of key.

Figure 6.2.

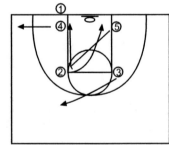

5 sets screen for 2 and cuts back down lane for ball. 2 comes off screen by 5 and cuts opposite side of basket. 4 pops out to wing, and 3 cuts to top of key.

Figure 6.3.

- Stack #1 (Refer to Figure 6.4)

- Stack #2 (Refer to Figure 6.5)

- Sideline (Refer to Figure 6.6)

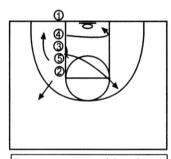

2 pops out to top of key. 3 sets screen for 5, who cuts towards basket for pass. 4 cuts across lane under basket.

Figure 6.4.

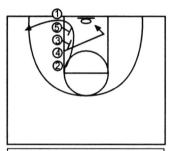

3 and 5 set a double screen for 2 to shoot. 4 cuts down lane to opposite block.

Figure 6.5.

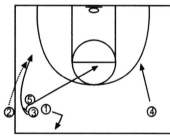

2 looks to see how 5 is guarded. If 5 is open to basket, she's the first option. Otherwise, 5 screens for 3, who looks for a quick pass. 1 pops up for safety pass, and 4 breaks to basket.

Figure 6.6.

LAST-SECOND PLAYS

The following examples are plays you could use for the special-situation drills. Each of these plays can be run in two to seven seconds.

- Full-court special #1 (Refer to Figure 6.7)
- Full-court special #2 (Refer to Figure 6.8)
- Full-court special #3 (Refer to Figure 6.9)
- 3/4 court special #1 (Refer to Figure 6.10)
- 3/4 court special #2 (Refer to Figure 6.11)
- 3/4 court special #3 (Refer to Figure 6.12)
- Half-court special #1 (Refer to Figure 6.13)
- Half-court special #2 (Refer to Figure 6.14)
- Half-court special #3 (Refer to Figure 6.15)

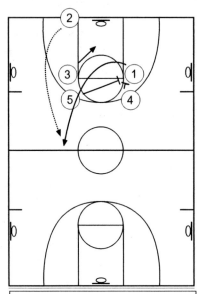

4 and 5 set a double screen for 1, who sprints to opposite basket looking for a long pass from 2. 3 trails.

Figure 6.7.

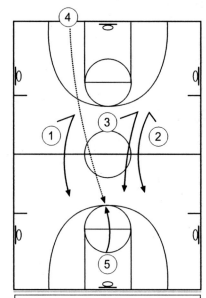

5 breaks up to top of key to receive pass from 4. 1, 2, and 3 fill the lanes and look for a tip from 5 if 5 can't receive the pass cleanly.

Figure 6.8.

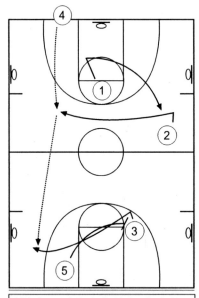

1 fakes towards the ball and goes back down sideline. 2 fakes up and then cuts hard across the court. 4 tries to get ball to 2 on the move. When 2 receives the ball, 5 screens for 3, who waits for a pass.

Figure 6.9.

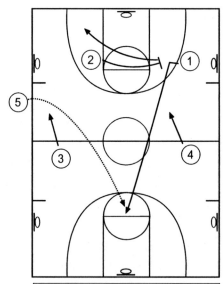

3 and 4 break hard to the ball. 2 pivots to set screen for 1 and rolls back. 1 cuts hard to screen, then goes deep looking for pass and easy lay-up.

Figure 6.10.

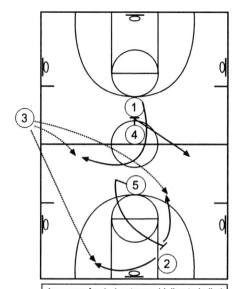

4 screens for 1. 1 cuts up sideline to ball. 4 rolls to opposite side of court. 5 screens for 2 and rolls back. 2 cuts off screen toward ball, and 3 passes to open player for shot.

Figure 6.11.

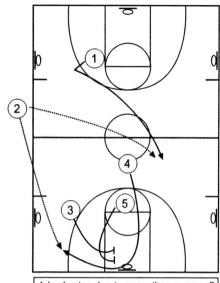

4 is shooter. 4 cuts away, then comes off double screen by 5 and 3. 1 steps to ball, then cuts backside. 2 looks to 4 and then to 1.

Figure 6.12.

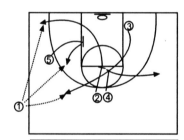

2 and 4 double screen down for 3. After setting screen, 2 continues to corner off screen by 5. 5 sets up at elbow after setting screen. 4 spots up to wing, 3 comes off double screen ready to shoot.

Figure 6.13.

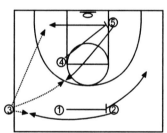

1 screens for 2, then fades. 4 down screens for 5 and rolls hard to corner. 5 cuts hard off the down screen to the elbow.

Figure 6.14.

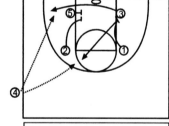

2 and 1 cut down to 5 and 3, 2 holds in double screen with 5.3 fakes up and cuts off double. 1 flashes to ballside elbow. 4 steps in for return pass and last second shot.

Figure 6.15.

QUICK-HITTERS

"Quick-hitters" are plays set apart from your normal offensive pattern. You might consider using them after a time-out, at the end of a quarter, or if you're behind by two points and are having trouble with a particular defense. Figures 6.16-6.18 illustrate three examples of quick-hitting plays.

- Three-point play (Refer to Figure 6.16)
- Junior high trick play (Refer to Figure 6.17)
- Double screen for two or three points (Refer to Figure 6.18)

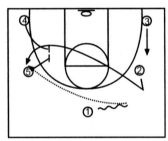

1 dribbles towards 2, who cuts to 1 as if to receive pass then runs around screen from 4 and 5 and sets up to shoot three-point shot.

Figure 6.16.

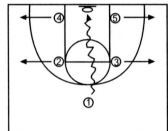

2, 3, 4, and 5 all start tight in lane, then on 1's command, all clear the lane to let 1 dribble in for one-one-one lay-up. Run against man-to-man and may only work once.

Figure 6.17.

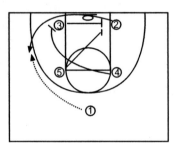

3 and 5 set a double screen down low for 2. 4 cuts down to opposite block for another screen for 2. 2 cuts off double screen, then single screen looking for pass from 1.

Figure 6.18.

Setting up in a 1-4 set also gives you numerous opportunities for a quick score. You can develop your own plays using single screens, double screens, entry passes to various players, and back-door cuts. Figures 6.19-6.24 illustrate several examples of quick-scoring plays.

POST ENTRY OPTIONS:

- #1 (Refer to Figure 6.19)
- #2 (Refer to Figure 6.20)
- #3 (Refer to Figure 6.21)

WING ENTRY OPTIONS:

- #1 (Refer to Figure 6.22)
- #2 (Refer to Figure 6.23)
- #3 (Refer to Figure 6.24)

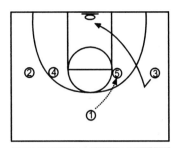

1 passes to 5. 3 cuts towards 1 to shake defender and cuts back door for a pass and open lay-up.

Figure 6.19.

1 passes to 5 and waits for a screen from 3. 5 can hand the ball off or pass it to 1 on the run.

Figure 6.20.

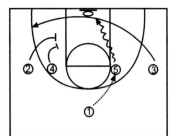

3 cuts to opposite side of court, using double screen from 4 and 5. 1 passes to 5. 5 waits for 3 to clear and dribbles in for shot.

Figure. 6.21.

1 passes to 3. 5 sets a screen for 4, who comes around for pass from 3.

Figure 6.22.

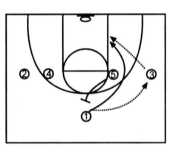

1 passes to 3, then waits for screen from 5. 3 passes to 1 for lay-up.

Figure 6.23.

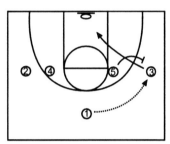

1 passes to 3 who waits for a screen from 5, then goes in for lay-up.

Figure 6.24.

THE STALL

This offense is a simple continuing offensive pattern to use if you are ahead and the other team needs to stop the clock (Refer to Figure 6.25). You might consider using one of your regular patterned offenses with the intent to stall without giving the ball away.

PRESS BREAKS

- #1 (Refer to Figure 6.26)
- #2 (Refer to Figure 6.27)
- #3 (Refer to Figure 6.28)
- #4 (Refer to Figure 6.29)

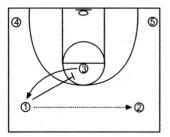
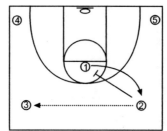
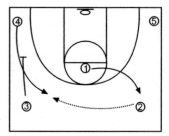

| Set up in a 2-1-2 set. 1 passes to 2 and then sets a screen for 3. | 2 passes back to 3 and sets a screen for 1. | If in trouble, 3 can set a down screen for 4, but only if 4 can handle the ball without a turnover. |

Figure 6.25.

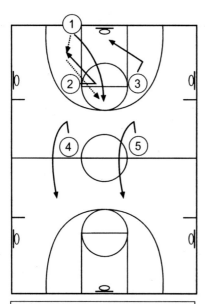

1 inbounds the ball and cuts to middle for a pass. 2 gets ball, dribbles down the sideline, and passes to 1 or 3. 4 and 5 cut up to help if needed, then run straight to basket, ready for a pass to set up offense.

Figure 6.26.

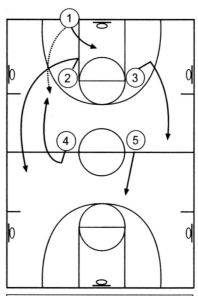

1 inbounds to 4 and stays as a safety. 4 looks to pass to 2 or 3 on the run. 5 sprints to basket.

Figure 6.27.

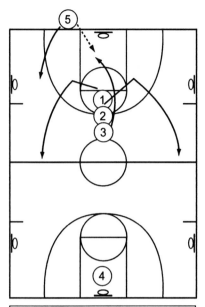

1, 2, and 3 line up in a stack at the free-throw line. 4 stays back to force a defender downcourt to cover her. 1 and 2 break up for the ball, then go hard down the sideline. 3 breaks up, gets pass, and looks for 1 or 2 on the run.

Figure 6.28.

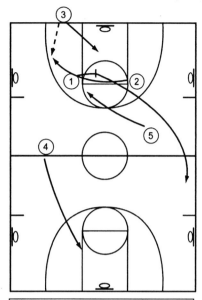

1 sets a screen for 2 then cuts downcourt. 2 goes to ball. 5 breaks up for pass from 2. 4 cuts down lane. 3 stays back to help. 5 is looking to pass to 1 or 4 on the run.

Figure 6.29.

FAST BREAKS

- #1 (Refer to Figure 6.30)
- #2 (Refer to Figure 6.31)
- #3 (Refer to Figure 6.32)

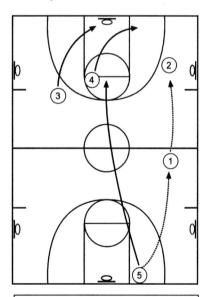

On a made basket 5 throws the ball to 1 who dribbles down the sideline looking for 2. 3 sprints to opp. block, 4 cuts across lane and slides to near block and 5 trails. 2 can shoot the 3, pass to 4 or wait for 5.

Figure 6.30.

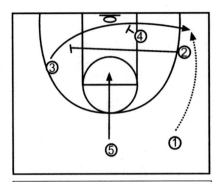

As 1 dribbles down floor, 2 cuts across and sets a screen for 3. 4 screens as well. Pass goes to 3 for shot.

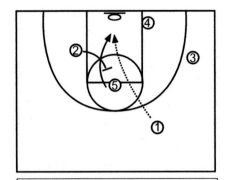

If 3 is not open, 2 screens for 5, who cuts down lane looking for a pass from 1.

Figure 6.31.

Figure 6.32.

Team Defense

MAN-TO-MAN (PERSON-TO-PERSON)

At any competitive level, it is important to emphasize the following points:

- Stay between your opponent and the basket.
- Do not turn your back to the ball.
- When the ball is two passes away, sag off your opponent towards the ball but know where your opponent is at all times to offer weak-side help.
- When the ball is one pass away, move back to guard your opponent.
- Do not let a player drive by you on the baseline or down the middle of the floor.
- Don't go too far out from the basket unless your team is in a half-court press.
- Force the ball away from the middle of the court – overplay the right side if the point guard favors her right hand.
- Keep a good distance from the offensive player you are guarding. Standing too close keeps you from reacting as quickly.
- As the player with the ball gets closer to the basket, you should guard her more closely.
- Communicate with each other when being screened.
- Once a player picks up her dribble, cover all passing lanes.

ZONES

A zone defense is a good place to start with a beginning-level team. It forces the other team to shoot from the outside, and it gives your team an advantage when rebounding. The following are the most popular zone defensive sets:

- 2-3 (Refer to Figure 7.1)
- 2-1-2 (Refer to Figure 7.2)
- 1-3-1 (Refer to Figure 7.3)
- Box-1 (Refer to Figure 7.4)
- Triangle-2 (Refer to Figure 7.5)

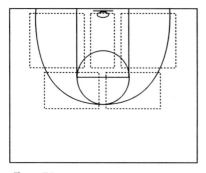

Figure 7.1.

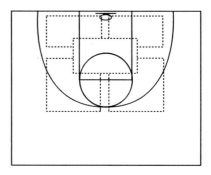

Figure 7.2.

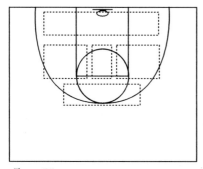

Figure 7.3.

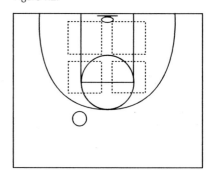

Figure 7.4.

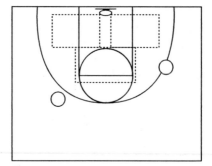

Figure 7.5.

PRESSES

You can pick up plenty of points using an aggressive, non-stop press. As a rule, such a press disrupts the offense of the opposing team. Because stopping a pass to the middle of the court is a main concern when pressing, you must emphasize directing play to the sideline. A man-to-man press works well if you incorporate some traps; otherwise, you're typically confronted by a one-on-one situation, where one good ball handler brings the ball down, and the rest of the team clears out.

- Full-court presses:

   2-2-1 (Refer to Figure 7.6)

   1-2-1-1 (Refer to Figure 7.7)

- Half-court press:

   1-3-1 (Refer to Figure 7.8)

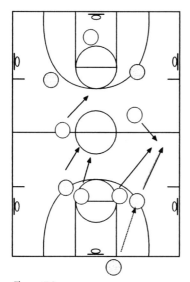

Figure 7.6.

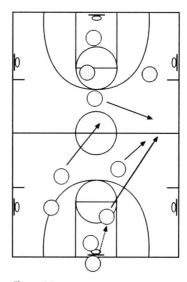

Figure 7.7.

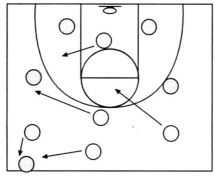

Figure 7.8.

INBOUNDS

A 2-3 zone is the best defense to use in this situation, whether you have been playing man-to-man or zone. A 2-3 zone on an inbounds play should prevent any cutters down low who are looking for an easy jumper from getting open; stop the player who inbounds the ball from getting a quick return pass for a 10-foot shot; and prevent a reverse for a possible three-point shot. You want to keep the opposition from getting a quick score by forcing a turnover or making them set up their offense.

FAST BREAK

At the moment the opposing team begins a fast break, the most important thing for your team to do is turn and run to the paint.

CHAPTER 8

Scouting

Live scouting is obviously more challenging than watching a film that you can stop, pause, and rewind. You should ask an assistant or a knowledgeable friend to go with you as you scout an upcoming opponent.

GENERAL CHECKLIST Use the form illustrated in Figure 8.1 as an example of a scouting form. Gather the following information:

❑ Get starting lineup, including names and numbers, if possible.

❑ Next to each starter, indicate strengths and weaknesses.

❑ Watch for substitutions – note who goes in for each player.

❑ Indicate weaknesses of substitutes.

❑ Find the "weak link" (e.g. a player who folds under pressure, can't dribble with left hand, won't shoot from the outside, etc.)

OFFENSIVE CHECKLIST:

❑ Press breaks

❑ Transition offense

❑ Inbounds plays (under opponent's basket, under their own basket, sideline)

❑ Half-court offense

❑ Shot chart (indicate a shot taken by writing the player's number at the spot of the shot, and circle her number if she makes the shot). Use the chart illustrated in Figure 8.2.

Teams:_____ vs. _____ Date:_____

Score by quarters:

Team	Q1	Q2	Q3	Q4	OT	Final

Out-of-Bounds Plays

Pass Offense

Transition Weaknesses

Offense

Defense

Starting lineup

No.	Name	Year	Grade	Strengths/Weaknesses/Stats

Substitutes

No.	Name	Year	Grade	Strengths/Weaknesses/Stats

Figure 8.1. Scouting form.

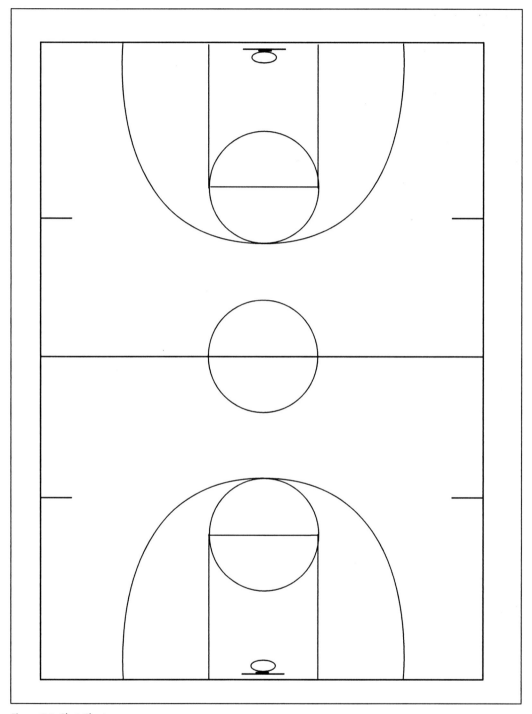

Figure 8.2. Shot Chart.

DEFENSIVE CHECKLIST:

- ❑ Are they in man-to-man?
- ❑ Do they switch on screens?
- ❑ Do they trap, leaving a player open?
- ❑ What zone are they playing?

AFTER THE GAME– Ask questions similar to what were asked in Chapter 2:

- ❑ Does the team have overall speed and quickness? (If so, then work on transition and zone defenses.)
- ❑ Do they have a great one-on-one player? (If so, then take your best defensive player and work on a box-1 defense.)
- ❑ Is the team skilled in ballhandling and able to penetrate? (If so, then use a zone defense, force them to shoot from the outside, watch backdoor cuts, and keep quick scores to a minimum.)
- ❑ Do they have good post players with superior height? (If so, then double-team best post player, deny passes into the lane.)
- ❑ What is their favorite offense, favorite defense, and favorite inbounds play? (Develop a game plan around these tendencies.)

Game-Day Considerations

DEVELOP A GAME PLAN

After scouting your opponent, it's time to decide on a plan of attack. Make a reference sheet so you have something helpful to look at during the heat of the moment. Include offenses to run against your opponent's favorite defense, some inbounds plays, and last-second plays. In the game-plan example illustrated in Figure 9.1, the same numbered offenses as those explained in Chapter Five are used. For your last-second plays, draw them out and staple them to your reference sheet in order to save time during a time-out. You can just flip to them when needed.

Defense:	Offense to counter:
2-3	#2, #3
1-3-1	#1, #4, #7
Box-1	#5a
Triangle-2	#5b, #5c
Man-to-man	#6, #8, #9
Quick-hitters:	**Inbounds plays:**
Post entry - option 1	Box 1
3-pt. play	Box 3
	Stack 1
	Sideline
Last-second plays:	
Full-court special #1	
3/4 court special #3	
Half-court special #1	

Figure 9.1. Game plan.

AWAY GAME PREPARATION

❏ *Uniform management* — Develop a system for handing out and collecting uniforms for an away game. Set them out about 30 minutes before departure time. Then after the game, the players should put their own uniform into the laundry bag. The managers should be responsible for getting the uniforms on the bus and then in the wash when back at school.

❏ *Trip items* — Although your managers should have a travel checklist, among the items you should include are the following:

- scorebook
- statistic sheets
- five balls
- water bottles
- towels

- extra uniform
- medicine kit
- video camera equipment
- roster with starters for announcer

HOME GAME PROCEDURES

- Sweep floor.
- Get clock ready.
- Set up scorer's table.
- Put out chairs for both teams.
- Make sure coaches' boxes are clearly outlined.
- Clean opponent's dressing room and make sure lockers are locked.
- Have a place for officials to dress before the game and a place for them to go during halftime.

PRE-GAME ROUTINE

Your routine should get the team warmed up and stretched so they feel comfortable and are ready to play. It doesn't have to be a well-choreographed show. They should get plenty of opportunities to shoot so they are familiar with the court. The following illustrates one possible pre-game routine that can be used:

- Run in with the first two players carrying a ball.
- Run a lap and a half.

- Two-line lay-ups, then jump shots.

- Four corners (or star drill)

- Three-man weave

- Guards go stretch, while the posts shoot.

- Switch after about three to four minutes.

- Line up for free throws.

- Huddle up, give last-minute instructions, and wait for the introduction of the team.

KEEPING STATS DURING THE GAME

Use your assistant coaches, managers, or knowledgeable parents to keep stats for you. Consider using the form illustrated in Figure 9.2.

❑ Shot chart — When a player shoots, record her number at the spot where she shot the ball. If she makes it, circle her number. Do this for both teams. You will get a visual picture of who is hurting you and from where.

❑ Stat sheet — You may need to change the statistics you keep to correspond to the statistics software program you are using. Most of the time, the software comes with its own stat sheet to alleviate this problem.

Your team vs. _____ Date: _____	Team		Q1	Q2	Q3	Q4	OT	Final

	Shots		Free throws		Rebounds				
#	Att.	Made	Att.	Made	Off.	Def.	Steals	Turnovers	Blocks

Figure 9.2. Stat sheet.

COACHING POINTS

❏ The First Half

As you watch the start of the game, make a quick analysis, so that during your first time-out, you can make adjustments, if necessary. Don't just watch the movement of the ball—be aware of the entire floor. Try to analyze play by answering the following questions:

- *Defense:* Are your players switching on screens? Are they letting opponents drive the baseline? Is there weak-side help when needed? Are they transitioning well?

- *Offense:* Are your players moving away from the ball? When running a patterned offense, what options are open? Are your players spaced well on the floor?

- *Opponent's defense:* Are they in a zone with an odd or even front? Are they playing man-to-man? Are they switching on screens? Are they using a full-court press or half-court press?

- *Opponent's offense:* Who is their main "go-to" player? What patterns are developing? Where are they scoring? (Post play, three-point shooting, backdoor cuts, etc.) Are there any automatics in transition? Does the point guard favor the left or right side? Where are they successful on the inbounds plays? Do they have any "quick-hitters"?

These are questions to keep in mind during the entire course of the game so you can make adjustments either during a time-out or during halftime. During that first time-out, be positive and give specific feedback. For example, "Susie, look for Amy on the left wing. She's wide open on such-and-such play."

❏ Halftime

As soon as you get into the locker room, settle the team down, encourage them, or challenge them. Check your scorebook and shot chart to evaluate the opponent's scoring. Talk to your players and give them instructions about adjustments you want to make, then have them go out and shoot. Structure your halftime so everyone has an opportunity to shoot. While the team is shooting, meet with your assistants and get input from them. Make changes, but be ready for the opposing team to make changes as well. Once you are ready to start the half, send your starters out to the positions illustrated in Figure 9.3.

If the opposing team does not realize which direction you are going, you have an easy lay-up. If they cover you correctly, then just have your team run back and inbound the ball. This works great at the junior high level, but it can occasionally work with varsity teams too. You can also run this at the start of a quarter. The only drawback is the officials will certainly mess this up for you, unless you warn them beforehand.

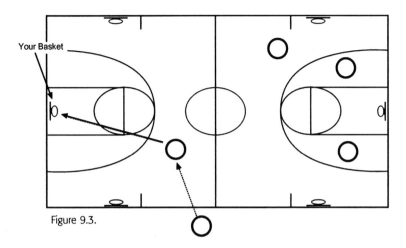

Your Basket

Figure 9.3.

❏ **The Second Half**

Right after the start of the half, see how well your team has responded to the adjustments and see what changes your opponent has made. You might need to call a time-out after only a few possessions to fix things. Keep an eye on the conditioning of your team as well. For extra rest, substitute for a tired player before the end of a quarter, giving her a little extra time.

MISCELLANEOUS GAME STUFF

- When a foul is called, pay attention to who was fouled so the wrong player is not sent to the line to shoot. Whoever committed the foul should also check so there is no chance of a mix-up.

- If you have a player who gets her third foul right after the second half begins, consider keeping her in the game rather than pulling her out for a significant time. You want to keep your best players in the game, so caution her to play with less aggression. Better players normally have a sense of how to avoid fouling when the game is on the line. This is certainly a subjective decision, but during a close game, you do want your best on the floor.

- During free throws on your half of the court, send a player back to defend any opposing player at half-court. If the free throw takes place on the opposing team's half, have at least one more player than they do under the basket to rebound.

- Instill in your team a respect for the officials, even though the officials may not be doing the best job. Interaction between players and officials should be kept to a minimum and restricted to only the team captain   when a discrepancy or question exists.

- Make adjustments when new players from the opposing team come into the game. In other words, your team should communicate to let everyone know who is guarding whom. When you send a substitute into the game, the player coming out should tell the substitute who she was guarding.

- Change strategy during breaks in the game. For example, substitute and change defenses after every time-out or after a free throw.

- When behind, foul to lengthen the game. Know the weakest free throw shooters on the opposing team.

- If you are behind and need two scores to win, look to score a quick two and then follow with a time-out.

- Remember it's just a game. (Easy to say, harder to do, right?)

AFTER THE GAME

Secure the scorebook and all basketballs immediately after the game, and then send the players to the locker room. Give them feedback and be positive, whether you won or lost. When you call in your scores to a local paper, have the following information ready:

- Your opponent and the final score.

- Score by quarters.

- All players who scored for your team and their point totals.

- The team's leader in rebounds or steals (so the emphasis isn't always on points).

- Your current team record.

- Which team you play next and where.

Have your managers start washing the uniforms, rinsing out water bottles, and putting the equipment away. You should stay with any players who are waiting for a ride, and then go put the bus away. Turn out all lights, lock up, and go home.

THE NEXT DAY

Enter your statistics into your computer program and post them for the team to see. Write a short newspaper article if you don't have a local sportswriter who covers your games.

CHAPTER 10

Season-Ending Responsibilities

EQUIPMENT MANAGEMENT

Collect all equipment and check for damaged items to repair or replace. Compile a list of needs for the next season with a cost analysis. Order equipment as soon as you can, to eliminate the hassle at the beginning of the next season (if your budget allows).

COLLEGE RECRUITING

Contact colleges and send information on graduating seniors who hope to compete at the collegiate level. Put together a highlight video for each senior to send to these colleges and be sure to include the athlete's name and school on the label of the video. Include her season and/or career statistics with the cover letter as well.

ASSEMBLING A YEARBOOK

This "yearbook" is something that can be as simple or elaborate as you want. The following items are examples of what you might include:

❑ **Front cover**

Consider using a team picture or a picture of the mascot on the front cover. Color obviously looks the best, but black and white looks fine as well. Refer to Figure 10.1 for an example of a front-cover layout.

❑ Table of contents

- School information
- Schedule
- Individual statistics
- Game statistics
- Season totals

- Team stats for season
- "Top five" list
- Newspaper articles
- All-district selections
- Letter to athletes

❑ School information sheet

Include a list of the district opponents, names of important administrators, the school address, mascot, and school colors (Refer to Figure 10.2.).

Figure 10.1. Sample front-cover layout.

Figure 10.2. Sample school information sheet.

❑ Individual statistics

Put the athlete's picture with a short paragraph describing her season accomplishments (Refer to Figure 10.3). The first example is of someone who played and the second is of someone who didn't:

Laura was a regular starter for us this season and did an excellent job at the point-guard position. She was the leading scorer, finishing the season with an 18.2 points-per-game average. The highlight of her season was the game-winning three-point shot to secure a win, and a trip to the playoffs. She is also on the "top five" list for steals and assists.

Sonya was a back-up guard this year and, when called upon, did an outstanding job. Her best performance was in the Mt. Pilot game, where she was three-for-three from the free-throw line, helping the team achieve a 67-62 victory. She made other great contributions, and will definitely see more action on the court next year.

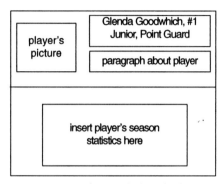

Figure 10.3. Sample individual profile sheet.

❑ "Top five" list

Rank players in the following categories — add more if you desire. (Refer to Figure 10.4):

- Total points
- Rebounds

- Steals
- Blocked shots

Figure 10.4. Sample team season leaders list.

Letter to athletes

Add a personal note to the back of the yearbook reflecting on the year and encouraging the returning members to work hard for next year. The following illustrates an example of such a personal note.

> *The dedication and hard work exhibited by the 2000-2001 women's varsity basketball team paid dividends beyond initial expectations. A team that consisted of primarily underclassmen excelled to the maximum potential by season's end. I am extremely proud of this group and anxiously look forward to next season.*
>
> *The opening game against Mayberry wasn't what we had hoped for, but as the season progressed, the skill level and confidence steadily improved. A playoff berth was a great accomplishment for this team and, with the majority of the players returning, the 2001-2002 season looks very promising. With continued hard work and dedication, our season looks to be a month longer next year!*
>
> *Work hard this summer, and remember, "Winners are ordinary people with extraordinary determination!"*
>
> *Sincerely,*
>
> *Coach Jordan*

BANQUET SPEECHES

You would think that since you are a teacher who speaks in front of a group on a regular basis, speaking at a sports banquet couldn't be that bad. To make things easier, keep one primary thing in mind — *be brief*. The following example illustrates a relatively brief banquet speech.

> **I'm so honored** *(even if you're not)* **to have the opportunity to present to you the 2002 Women's Basketball Team. We finished the season with a record of _____ and ended up _____ place in the district.**
>
> *(Discuss any great wins or playoff experiences here.)*
>
> **I would now like to present to you the MVP of the season. She led the team in scoring, rebounding, and blocked shots. She is dedicated to the sport and is an exceptional athlete, leader, and student. The award goes to**
>
> _____ .

ALL-DISTRICT/ALL-CONFERENCE/ALL-LEAGUE SELECTIONS

When it is time to meet with your colleagues and decide on All-District selections, there are two meeting formats you might encounter. If you are in charge of the meeting, you might want to use one of the following methods:

❏ **"Traditional" Method**

Major awards should be voted on first (e.g., most valuable player, newcomer of the year, defensive player of the year, offensive player of the year). Those who receive one of the major awards are then eliminated from the rest of the voting to give other athletes an opportunity to be nominated. Coaches are not allowed to vote for their own players.

After the major awards have been given, the coaches should decide on how many athletes will be on the first-team list. (For example, six guards and six post players.) Nominations are then taken for guards. One person at the board should write down all the nominations from each coach with the following information:

Name	School	Position	Classification

When all the nominations are made, each coach votes for five players. Coaches may not vote for their own athlete. These votes can be made on any type of note-taking paper, including scraps of paper. The results are then tallied on the board. The top five vote-getters are the first-team selections. If a tie occurs, you may revote to break the tie or the coaches may mutually agree to add the extra player.

The names left on the board who were not selected for first team may be left on the board to be considered for second-team selection. Any additional spots can be filled by new nominations and a vote. You can also choose to erase the board and start the nominating process all over. Once the voting is complete, coaches may then add whomever they want to the honorable-mention selections without a group vote.

❏ **"Alternative" Method**

This procedure involves voting on the major awards, which again eliminates those athletes from the rest of the nominating process. In this instance, each coach is allowed a pre-determined number of first- and second-team selections based on where they finished as a team in the district. The coach makes the decision who receives which honor. The following example of this process involves a district with six teams and 12 spots for first team and 12 spots for second team:

- First place team gets six picks – three for first team and three for second team

- Second place team gets five picks – three for first team and two for second team

- Third place team gets four picks – two for first team and two for second team
- Fourth place team gets three picks – two for first team and one for second team
- Fifth place team gets two picks – one for first team and one for second team
- Sixth place team gets one pick – one for first team or one for second team

This system works well, and each coach gets exactly who they want on each team. Honorable mention is done the same way as the traditional method.

SUMMER LEAGUE ORGANIZATION

Starting a summer league program can give your girls valuable game experience. Among the steps to get started are the following:

- Get approval from the administration to use the facilities for games and practices.
- Find some responsible adult volunteers to coach your team.
- Have your high school girls sign up and pay a fee that should cover insurance, jerseys, and officials.
- Talk with surrounding schools to set up a league schedule.
- Schedule several tournaments during the summer. These will be an additional cost for the girls so let them know up front. Entry fees usually run from $100 - $250 per team.
- Order reversible jerseys for each player.
- Consider including younger grades if you have plenty of volunteer coaches.
- Meet with your volunteers to schedule practices. This step will help avoid conflicts when using the facilities.

Off-Season Training

PLANNING

Reflect on the season, look over your practices, watch game film, and study your season statistics, and then decide what your team's weaknesses were and how you on can improve on them. It might be conditioning, strength, or offensive production. Whatever it is, concentrate on that weakness during the off-season. The off-season is also a good time to reinforce basic fundamentals.

OFF-SEASON ACTIVITIES

The off-season should be geared to a basic enhancement of physical fitness, including improvement in speed, agility, and strength. Divide your off-season into three phases: general, intermediate, and concentrated (or phase one, phase two, and phase three). Among the types of activities that should be included in your off-season program are the following:

❑ **Speed drills:**

- A2's – This drill is similar to a skipping motion but with emphasis on good sprint mechanics. Instead of skipping with a straight leg, the thigh comes up to parallel with the ground. The foot should also be parallel to the ground rather than hanging down as if pointing the toe. The emphasis should be placed on getting as many contacts on the ground in the required distance.

- B2's – Also known as a pawing drill, the mechanics are similar to the A2. After driving the knee, the foot should kick out, so the leg is extended and parallel to the ground. At this point, the foot should be pulled down to the ground in a pawing action, striking the ground under the body.

- Heel-ups – This is similar to what we all know as "butt kicks." The heels just need to come high under the body in a quick cycle. Again, emphasize quickness and making contact with the ground as many times as possible in a short distance.

- Flying 10's, 20's, and 30's – Measure twice the distance you want the athlete to "fly" (in meters). Place cones at the start, at the middle, and at the end of the run. The first half of the run should be for a gradual acceleration. Once at the halfway point, the athlete should be running at full speed and should maintain that speed until the end of the run.

❑ Plyometrics:

- Double-leg bound – Jump outward and upward, using forward thrusting movements of the arms with no pause between jumps.

- Alternate-leg bound – This exercise involves an exaggerated running motion. Start the athletes at a jog and gradually get them to drive their knees up towards the chest. The idea is to gain as much height and distance as possible.

- Single-leg bound – Hop with one leg at a time, also trying to gain as much height and distance as possible.

- Squat jump – Jump up and down continuously, using a full squatting motion when on the ground.

- Tuck jump – This jump is also up and down, but the emphasis is on bringing the knees to the chest at the height of the jump.

- Scissor jump – Start in a lunge position and jump as high and straight in the air as possible, using the arms to gain lift. At the top of the jump, the legs are reversed before landing.

❑ Dummy drills

Set up the dummies as shown in Figure 11.1, and work on the following drills:

- High knees – Run over the bags, using high-knee action.

- Lateral step – Face sideways and lead with the right foot over the first bag. Both feet should meet in the middle, and the right foot should be ready to lead again. Switch directions going back so the left leg leads.

- Sprint – Run through the bags, planting the outside foot at each one and sprinting to the next.

- Forward/backward – Facing sideways, run forward to the end of the first bag, backpedal to the next in a good defensive stance, and then go forward. Repeat with all four bags.

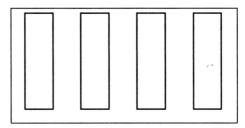

Figure 11.1. Dummy set-up for dummy drills.

❑ **Jump rope routines**

Make sure the jump rope is the appropriate length for each athlete. Measure from the tops of the athlete's feet to her armpit. Work each of the following exercises for 30 seconds.

- Both feet single jumps
- Right foot single jumps
- Left foot single jumps
- Both feet side to side over a line
- Both feet front and back over a line
- Two jumps left foot – two jumps right foot – single jumps
- Right foot side to side over a line
- Left foot side to side over a line
- Right foot front and back over a line
- Left foot front and back over a line
- Both feet three single jumps – one double jump
- Both feet consecutive double jumps

❑ **Medicine ball drills:**

- Squat throw – Bend down in a squatting position with the medicine ball between the legs. Explode upward, throwing the ball in the air. Upon catching it, squat immediately and repeat the sequence.

- Trunk twist – Two athletes stand back to back with one medicine ball. As athlete #1 turns to the right to pass the ball, athlete #2 turns left to receive it. Athlete #2 then quickly turns to pass to her right while athlete #1 receives the ball from her left. Rotate after 10-20 reps.

- Sit-up throw – Two athletes sit on the floor facing each other with their legs locked. Athlete #1 holds the ball above her head, while athlete #2 is sitting, waiting to receive the ball. Athlete #1 lays backward, comes up and throws to athlete #2. Athlete #2 receives the ball and bends backward to absorb the shock of the throw, thereby engaging the abdominal muscles. As athlete #2 comes forward, she throws to athlete #1, who also receives the ball, bends backward, and absorbs the shock. The pattern continues for 10-20 reps.

- Chest pass – Two athletes should be on their knees about 6-8 feet apart facing each other. The ball is pushed rapidly by one athlete to another, extending arms completely.

- Overhead pass – Two athletes should stand 10-12 feet apart and using an overhead passing motion, pass the ball back and forth to each other.

❏ **Weight training**

Start the weight training program by "maxing out" on the core lifts: bench, squat, dead lift, and hang cleans. The resultant data will give you an idea of who should be grouped together. There should be three in each group so that one athlete is lifting, one is spotting, and one is working on a supplemental lift. Each group will rotate through the core lifts and wait for the other groups to finish.

Demand precision and discipline in the weight room so that no one gets injured. Have the athletes stand at their current station until everyone is finished. When everyone is standing, break it down and move to the next station, keeping everyone on the same pace.

The following stations, with the core lift noted first, are recommended:

- *Squat*, calf raises
- Alternate these exercises:
  - ✓ *Bench*, incline flyes
  - ✓ *Incline*, flat-bench flyes
- *Dead lift*, crunches
- *Hang cleans*, hamstring curls, leg extensions (since a spotter isn't necessary, you can utilize two supplemental lifts)
- *Hip flexibility* (each group of three players steps over and under the five hurdles until everyone else is finished)

Figure 11.2 Illustrates an example of a weight room layout.

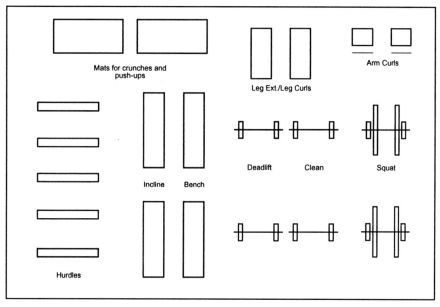

Figure 11.2. Weight room layout.

❏ Gym day circuits

On specified day, the players engage in a series of activities that are grouped by function into either a conditioning circuit or a fundamentals circuit.

- *Conditioning circuit:*

✓ Station 1 – Crunches

✓ Station 2 – Push-ups

✓ Station 3 – Jump rope

✓ Station 4 – Step ups

✓ Station 5 – Jogging

✓ Station 6 – Speed weights or medicine ball drills

✓ Station 7 – Defensive mirror drill

✓ Station 8 – Dummies

- *Fundamentals circuit* (Refer to Figure 11.3):

✓ Station 1 – Dribbling drills

✓ Station 2 – Ballhandling drills

✓ Station 3 – Lay-ups

✓ Station 4 – Free throws

✓ Station 5 – One-on-one dribbling

✓ Station 6 – Stamina shooting drill

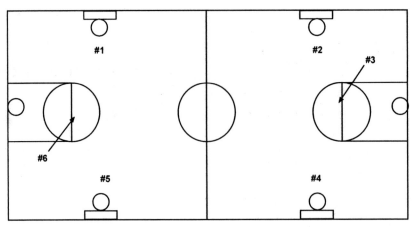

Figure 11.3.

❏ Competition-day activities

Another off-season program that can be used to develop your players involves having your athletes compete against each other in a series of games and drills, collectively referred to as competition-day activities. To make competition days more interesting, have your assistant coaches pick as many teams as the number of players on your team and the activities chosen dictate. Drafting players is recommended in order to ensure a fair distribution of talent. Coaches draw for first, second, third, etc, and pick according to the number of teams and coaches you have. The following example illustrates the drafting order for four teams:

	Round 1	Round 2	Round 3	Round 4
Team #1	first pick	fourth pick	third pick	second pick
Team #2	second pick	first pick	fourth pick	third pick
Team #3	third pick	second pick	first pick	fourth pick
Team #4	fourth pick	third pick	second pick	first pick

Note: The drafting order starts over again in round 5.

Keep a running total of scores until the end of the year in order to crown a winning team. Assign point totals for first, second, third, and fourth place (10, eight, five, and three points). Choose games and relays that are not only competitive, but athletically challenging as well. The following relays and games are designed for teams of eight players.

- *Relays*

Relay #1.

Set-up: Run this relay on a track. Athletes are stationed at locations on the track as illustrated in Figure 11.4.

Directions: Team members can decide who will run the following distances: 400m, 200m, 100m, 100m, repeat. Use a relay baton (or possibly something more cumbersome to add a measure of fun/entertainment to the relay).

Relay #2.

Set-up: Run this relay on a football field.

Directions: Team members must determine who will do the following: run 50 yards, wheelbarrow for 50 yards, switch and continue for another 50 yards, crab walk for 50 yards, bear crawl 50 yards, piggyback 50 yards, switch and continue for another 50 yards, run 50 yards.

Relay #3.

Set-up: The relay requires 10 cones, 10 hurdles, 12 tires, two soccer balls, and a sheet of plastic for an optional "water slide." The set-up for the relay is illustrated in Figure 11.5.

Directions: Run two teams at once and time them. Instead of using a relay baton, just have athletes the slap hands.

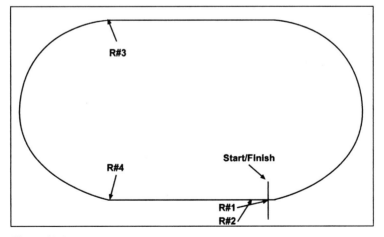

Figure 11.4.

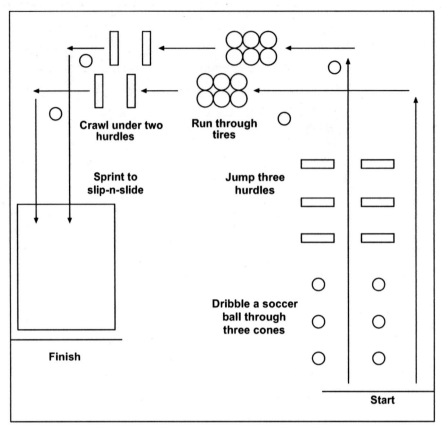

Figure 11.5.

- *Games*

Game #1.   Ultimate football:

Set-up: This game is played on a football field, using the width—not the entire length—of the field. Use cones and the end zone as boundaries.

Directions: The ball may only be advanced by throwing or pitching it. An athlete may not run forward with the ball, only sideways and backwards. If the ball hits the ground, the ball immediately goes to the other team. Play does not stop unless a touchdown is scored. A team scores by catching the ball in the end zone. If the ball is dropped, no points are scored, and possession reverts to the other team. Play for four quarters or two halves.

Game #2   Ballistic basketball:

Set-up: The game involves using either four goals, two goals, or just one goal and either one or two balls.

Directions: While regular basketball rules apply, you have four teams on the court at one time with the following guidelines/stipulations:

- Play to 10 points; the winning team must win by two points.

- After a basket is scored, the team in last place gets the ball, even if they just scored. If play stops for a violation, award the losing team the ball as well.

- Four-basket play – use the four side goals

- Two-basket play – use the regular goals

- One basket play – this may be tough with four teams of five, so use this option only if you play with teams of two or three players.

SETTING INDIVIDUAL GOALS

Have your athletes decide on how much they will increase their strength maxes, vertical jump, speed, etc. during the course of the off-season and keep a record of their chosen goals, as well as their test-evaluation performances, on their workout sheet. Test each athlete in the following areas:

- Strength – squat, hang clean, dead lift, bench press, dips, pull-ups

- Speed – 40-yard run (football does it, why can't you?)

- Quickness and agility – backpedal to the free-throw line, sprint to half-court, slide along the half-court line, backpedal to the free-throw line, and sprint to the baseline (Figure 11.6).

- Vertical jump

- 800-meter run (tested on a track)

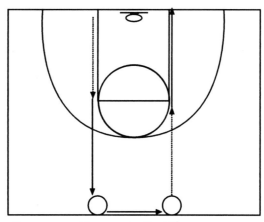

Figure 11.6. Quickness and agility drill.

OFF-SEASON SCORING CHART

Use the following charts (Tables 11.1 to 11.9) to award point values. Instead of giving points for first, second, third, etc., assign points based on performance. Although you may find this system somewhat different, it gives your athletes the ability to compete against themselves rather than someone else's best performance (as in the tryout evaluation). Consider it an off-season decathlon. Keep records in each event and total points for posterity.

❑ Squat

Weight	Pts.	Weight	Pts.	Weight	Pts.
300	1000	245	816	190	633
295	982	240	799	185	616
290	966	235	783	180	599
285	949	230	766	175	583
280	932	225	749	170	566
275	916	220	733	165	549
270	899	215	716	160	533
265	882	210	699	155	516
260	866	205	683	150	499
255	849	200	667	145	483
250	833	195	649	140	466

Table 11.1. Point values for the squat. Note: multiply the amount of weight lifted by 3.3, if that weight is not on the chart.

❑ Bench press

Weight	Pts.	Weight	Pts.	Weight	Pts.
160	1000	125	781	90	563
155	969	120	750	85	531
150	938	115	719	80	500
145	906	110	688	75	469
140	875	105	656	70	438
135	844	100	625	65	406
130	813	95	594	60	375

Table 11.2. Point values for the bench press. Note: Multiply the amount of weight lifted by 6.25, if that weight is not on the chart.

❏ Hang clean

Weight	Pts.	Weight	Pts.	Weight	Pts.
200	1000	155	775	110	550
195	975	150	750	105	525
190	950	145	725	100	500
185	925	140	700	95	475
180	900	135	675	90	450
175	875	130	650	85	425
170	850	125	625	80	400
165	825	120	600	75	375
160	800	115	575	70	350

Table 11.3. Point values for the hang clean. Note: Multiply the weight lifted by 5.0, if that weight it not on the chart.

❏ Dead lift

Weight	Pts.	Weight	Pts.	Weight	Pts.
250	1000	205	820	160	640
245	980	200	800	155	620
240	960	195	780	150	600
235	940	190	760	145	580
230	920	185	740	140	560
225	900	180	720	135	540
220	880	175	700	130	520
215	860	170	680	125	500
210	840	165	660	120	480

Table 11.4. Point values for the dead lift. Note: Multiply the weight lifted by 4.0 if that weight is not on the chart.

❑ Dips

No.	Pts.	No.	Pts.	No.	Pts.
15	1000	10	667	5	334
14	934	9	600	4	267
13	867	8	534	3	200
12	800	7	467	2	133
11	734	6	400	1	67

Table 11.5. Point values for dips. Note: Multiply the amount of dips performed by 66.7, if that number is not on the chart.

❑ Pull-ups

No.	Pts.	No.	Pts.	No.	Pts.
15	1000	10	667	5	334
14	934	9	600	4	267
13	867	8	534	3	200
12	800	7	467	2	133
11	734	6	400	1	67

Table 11.6. Point values for pull-ups. Note: Multiply the number of pull-ups performed by 66.7, if that number is not on the chart.

❑ 40-yard sprint

Time	Pts.	Time	Pts.	Time	Pts.
4.2	1000	4.9	720	5.6	440
4.3	960	5.0	680	5.7	400
4.4	920	5.1	640	5.8	360
4.5	880	5.2	600	5.9	320
4.6	840	5.3	560	6.0	280
4.7	800	5.4	520	6.1	240
4.8	760	5.5	480	6.2	200

Table 11.7. Point values for the 40-yard sprint. Note: Add or subtract 40 points (depending on the time achieved), if that time is not on the chart.

❏ Vertical jump

Inches	Pts.		Inches	Pts.		Inches	Pts.
33	1000		26	788		19	576
32	970		25	757		18	545
31	939		24	727		17	515
30	909		23	697		16	485
29	879		22	667		15	454
28	848		21	636		14	424
27	818		20	606		13	394

Table 11.8. Point values for the vertical jump. Note: Multiply the number of inches by 30.3, if that number is not on the chart.

❏ 800m run

Time	Pts.		Time	Pts.		Time	Pts.		Time	Pts.
2:45	1000		3:00	850		3:15	700		3:30	550
2:46	990		3:01	840		3:16	690		3:31	540
2:47	980		3:02	830		3:17	680		3:32	530
2:48	970		3:03	820		3:18	670		3:33	520
2:49	960		3:04	810		3:19	660		3:34	510
2:50	950		3:05	800		3:20	650		3:35	500
2:51	940		3:06	790		3:21	640		3:36	490
2:52	930		3:07	780		3:22	630		3:37	480
2:53	920		3:08	770		3:23	620		3:38	470
2:54	910		3:09	760		3:24	610		3:39	460
2:55	900		3:10	750		3:25	600		3:40	450
2:56	890		3:11	740		3:26	590		3:41	440
2:57	880		3:12	730		3:27	580		3:42	430
2:58	870		3:13	720		3:28	570		3:43	420
2:59	860		3:14	710		3:29	560		3:44	410

Table 11.9. Point values for the 800M run. Note: Add or subtract 10 points (depending on the time achieved), if that time is not on the chart.

❑ Agility run

Time	Pts.	Time	Pts.	Time	Pts.
6.0	1000	6.8	680	7.6	360
6.1	960	6.9	640	7.7	320
6.2	920	7.0	600	7.8	280
6.3	880	7.1	560	7.9	240
6.4	840	7.2	520	8.0	200
6.5	800	7.3	480	8.1	160
6.6	760	7.4	440	8.2	120
6.7	720	7.5	400	8.3	80

Table 11.10. Point values for the agility run. Note: Add or subtract 40 points (depending on the time achieved), if that time is not on the charts.

A SAMPLE OFF-SEASON CONDITIONING PROGRAM

Although weight lifting is essential for a well-rounded off-season, it may be difficult to schedule the weight room at a time that works well for your team (i.e., you don't have to share it with another group), or find time to get to the strength training facility during a relatively brief athletic period. Try to emphasize gaining strength during the summer by sending a summer program home with each of your athletes and opening the weight room for their use. The following conditioning program can be used in the months preceding the summer. A summer workout program is included later in this chapter.

❑ Phase One (March)

Develop a good conditioning base during this phase by focusing on slower, longer runs with less rest between sets. Spend at least one day in the gym during this phase to work on fundamentals. Add gym days in subsequent phases. Use circuits to focus on either a single skill or to incorporate several skills in the activity simultaneously.

SAMPLE WEEK:

Monday —

- Warm-up
- 6 x 200 meters @ 50% of maximum speed (walk 200 meters for rest)
- Weights: 3 x 10 @ 50% of max on core lifts; 3 x 12 on supplemental lifts

Tuesday

- Gym day

Wednesday

- Warm-up
- 20 diagonals on football field (Note: running a diagonal, then walking the width of the end-zone equals one repetition of the activity)
- Weights: 3 x 8 @ 65% of max; 3 x 12 on supplemental lifts

Thursday

- Warm-up
- Speed drills: 3 x 30m
- Dummy drills
- Plyometrics: 3 x 30m or 3 x 10 for stationary jumps

Friday

- Warm-up
- 10 x 100 meters @ 50% of maximum speed (run the length of a football field, then walk back)
- Weights: 3 x 10 @ 50% of max; 3 x 12 on supplemental lifts

❑ **Phase Two** (April)

Test strength maxes, times, jumps, etc. to assess an athlete's progress before beginning this phase.

SAMPLE WEEK:

Monday

- Warm-up
- 6 x 150 meters @ 70% of maximum speed with two minutes rest
- Dummy drills
- Weights: 3 x 8 @ 70%, 3 x 12 on supplemental lifts

Tuesday

- Gym day

Wednesday

- Warm-up
- Four sets of 10-, 20-, 30-meter "flies" @ 90% with one-minute rest between each set
- Plyometrics
- Weights: 3 x 8 @ 70%, 3 x 12 on supplemental lifts

Thursday

- Gym day

Friday

- Warm-up
- 12 x 50 yards on grass @ 70%, walk 50 yards back for rest
- Speed drills
- Weights: 3 x 8 @ 70%, 3 x 12 on supplemental lifts

❑ **Phase Three** (May)

Stay with a schedule calling for two days a week in the gym, but add one day of competition and test max performances one more time.

SAMPLE WEEK:

Monday

- Warm-up
- Speed drills
- Dummy drills
- Weights: 3 x 8 @ 70%, 3 x 12 on supplemental lifts

Tuesday

- Gym day

Wednesday

- Warm-up
- Four sets of 10-, 20-, 30-meter flies @ 90% with one minute rest
- Plyometrics
- Weights: 3 x 8 @ 70%, 3 x 12 on supplemental lifts

Thursday

- Gym day

Friday

- Competition day

SUMMER WORKOUT

You can spend a great deal of time building strength, stamina, speed, and agility, but unless your athletes are committed to a summer program, it's all lost. Before school lets out, give your athletes a workout manual, a weight-room schedule, and an open-gym schedule. Remind them that they will have to run 800m the first day of practice —a step that might help motivate some of them to workout more religiously. You may consider using some of the circuit programs for your gym days as well.

SUMMER WORKOUT MANUAL*

❏ Introduction

The following workout program is designed to help you maintain the conditioning, speed, and strength you worked hard to improve during the off-season. The workout will start the first week in June and will continue until the first week of school. This schedule averages out to about a 10-week period.

The entire program will consist of strength training, shooting drills, circuit training, and a running workout. Each part of the program is fully explained in this manual. At the end of the manual, you will find a training log divided into weeks with sets, reps, times, distances, etc. for you to follow.

❏ Weight program (if weight facility is accessible)

The weight program is based on your final max of the year. For core lifts, you will be working five sets starting with 10 reps, then 8, 6, 4, and 2 reps. The amount of weight to lift for each set can be determined by these simple steps. Using the max weight, take 50% of your max performance to determine your 10-rep poundage. Take 60% of the max weight to get the 8-rep poundage, and so on. For example, if your squat max is 220 lbs, the number of reps you would perform on each of the five sets would be as follows:

- First set: $220 \times .5 = 110$ lbs x 10 reps
- Second set: $220 \times .6 = 130$ lbs x 8 reps
- Third set: $220 \times .7 = 155$ lbs x 6 reps
- Fourth set: $220 \times .8 = 175$ lbs x 4 reps
- Fifth set: $220 \times .9 = 200$ lbs x 2 reps

*Note: The remainder of this chapter provides a sample summer workout manual.

123

A sample two-week schedule for performing the squat would involve the following reps and levels of resistance:

Monday	Thursday	Monday	Thursday
10 x 110 lbs	10 x 110 lbs	10 x 120 lbs	10 x 120 lbs
8 x 130 lbs	8 x 130 lbs	8 x 140 lbs	8 x 140 lbs
6 x 155 lbs	6 x 155 lbs	6 x 160 lbs	6 x 160 lbs
4 x 175 lbs	4 x 175 lbs	4 x 180 lbs	4 x 180 lbs
2 x 200 lbs	2 x 200 lbs	2 x 205 lbs	2 x 205 lbs

❑ Spacing your workouts

You can do upper body exercises one day and lower body exercises the next, or combine all of the required lifts in one day. Whichever option you choose, make sure you complete the core lifts (noted in italics). Supplemental lifts can be done as time allows. The following examples illustrates two routines that can be performed over the course of a week-long period.

- **Four-day split:**

Monday: *Bench*, military press, arm curls, upright rows, close-grip bench, push-ups, crunches

Tuesday: *Squat, hang clean*, stiff-legged dead lift, leg curls, leg extensions, calf raises, step-ups, lunges

Wednesday: Rest

Thursday: *Incline*, military press, arm curls, upright rows, close grip bench, push-ups, crunches

Friday: *Squat, snatch, or dead lift*, stiff-legged dead lift, leg curls, leg extensions, calf raises, step-ups, lunges

- **Two-day split:**

Monday: *Bench, squat, hang clean*, military press, arm curls, upright rows, close-grip bench, push-ups, crunches, leg curls, leg extensions, calf raises

Thursday: *Incline, squat, snatch, or dead lift*, military press, arm curls, upright rows, close-grip bench, push-ups, crunches leg curls, leg extensions, calf raises

❑ **Basketball drills:**

- Free throws: Shoot 50 at a time and increase that number to 100 by end of summer.

- Shooting off the dribble: Do each movement drill 10 times, then go left-handed:
    - ✓ shot fake – dribble right/left – shoot
    - ✓ shot fake – dribble right/left – crossover – shoot
    - ✓ shot fake – dribble right/left – between the legs dribble – shoot
    - ✓ shot fake–dribble right/left – behind the back dribble–crossover–shoot
    - ✓ shot fake – dribble right/left – spin move – one dribble – shoot

- Set shots: Take 20 shots from six positions on the court.

- Big man drill: Make a lay-up with the right hand, rebound, shoot with left hand, and continue for one minute. Rest one minute and continue drill. Work at least five minutes.

- Ballhandling:
    - ✓ single leg circle – both legs
    - ✓ figure eight drill – switch directions
    - ✓ cross-over dribbling – right, right, left, left
    - ✓ around body – switch directions
    - ✓ butterfly
    - ✓ pound dribble
    - ✓ dribble walk
    - ✓ full-court dribble – speed
    - ✓ zigzag dribble – work crossover and behind-the-back full speed

- Post moves (first on the right side of the lane, then the left):
    - ✓ low post moves (on block)
        - – flip ball to self – step back with left foot – power dribble – shoot
        - – flip ball to self – pivot to face basket – shoot
        - – flip ball to self – fake left – go right with dribble – shoot
        - – flip ball to self – fake right – pivot to basket – shoot

✓ high post moves (at elbow)

    —   flip ball to self – shot fake – drive right

    —   flip ball to self – shot fake – drive left

    —   flip ball to self – take step to right – pull-up jumper

    —   flip ball to self – take step to left – pull-up jumper

❏ Circuit programs

- Weight Circuit: (Note:If you are unable to get to a weight room, perform the following circuit.)

  ✓ Wall sits – Sit against the wall with your legs at 90-degree angles, back flat, and hands at sides for 45 seconds at a time.

  ✓ Chair dips – Using two chairs, put your feet on one chair and your palms on the other, with your arms behind your back. Lower yourself toward the floor with your arms at 90 degrees, then push back up. Repeat for three sets of 10.

  ✓ Push-ups – Perform regular straight leg push-ups for three sets of 10.

  ✓ Toe raises – Balance with one hand against the wall and raise one heel at a time for three sets of 25 (each leg).

  ✓ Lunges – Over a distance of about 30 yards for each set, perform three sets of lunges (alternating legs).

- Jump Rope Circuit: (Note: Do each station for 30 seconds and increase the time you spend at each station to one minute by summer's end.)

  ✓ Both feet single jumps

  ✓ Right foot single jumps

  ✓ Left foot single jumps

  ✓ Both feet side to side over a line

  ✓ Both feet front and back over a line

  ✓ Two jumps left foot – two jumps right foot – single jumps

  ✓ Right foot side to side over a line

  ✓ Left foot side to side over a line

  ✓ Right foot front and back over a line

  ✓ Left foot front and back over a line

✓ Both feet three single jumps – one double jump

✓ Both feet consecutive double jumps:

- Abdominal Circuit:

  ✓ Slide ups – Lay on your back with your arms rested on your thighs (palms down). Raise your back and shoulders off the ground and slide your hands to your knees. When your hands touch your knees, slowly slide back. (3 x 20)

  ✓ Obliques – Lay on your back with your arms behind your head. Have a partner hold on to your arms. Lift both legs so the bottoms of your feet are pointing to the ceiling. Lower your legs to the right so that your right leg touches the ground, then repeat the procedure to the left. Keep both feet together. (3 x 10)

  ✓ Crunches – Lay on your back with your knees bent and your hands over your chest. Raise your shoulders off the floor and back down. For a variation, rest your legs on a bench or lift them off the floor. (3 x 25)

  ✓ Reverse sit-ups – Lay on your back with your legs in the air so that the bottoms of your feet are pointing at the ceiling. Slowly raise your pelvis and lower back off the floor and then back down in a controlled manner. Do not rock; use just your pelvis muscles. (3 x 10)

  ✓ V-sits – Lay on your back with your arms over your head and your legs straight. At the same time, bring your arms and legs up and try to touch your feet above the center of your body. Then lower them both slowly. (3 x 10)

- Plyometric Circuit: (Note: Do this circuit on grass and work each exercise three times for 30 yards.)

  ✓ Double leg bound – Jump outward and upward using forward thrusting movements of your arms with no pause between jumps.

  ✓ Alternate leg bound – This exercise involves an exaggerated running motion. Start at a jog and gradually drive your knees up towards your chest. The idea is to gain as much height and distance as possible.

  ✓ Single leg bound – Hop with one leg at a time, also trying to gain as much height and distance as possible.

  ✓ Squat jump – Jump up and down continuously, using a full squatting motion when on the ground.

  ✓ Tuck jump – This jump is also up and down, but the emphasis is on bringing your knees to your chest at the height of the jump.

  ✓ Scissor jump – Start in a lunge position and jump as high and straight in the air as possible, using your arms to gain lift; at the top of the jump, reverse your legs before landing.

- Bleacher Circuit:

Run up and down the bleachers. Make sure you watch your step on the way up and down. Sprint up the stairs, but walk slowly as you come down to ensure good footing and to take stress off your knees.

Version #1:   Sprint to the top, one step at a time, and walk down slowly. Do this for 10 minutes of continuous running, using the walk down as the recovery.

Version #2:   If you are running stairs at a football stadium, start at the far left, sprint up, and walk back down the same way you came. Jog to the middle of the bleachers, sprint up, walk down the same way. Jog to the far right, sprint up, walk down, and then jog down out of the bleacher area (or walk if there are steps). Jog under the bleachers to your starting point at the far left of the bleachers. Perform this circuit five times and increase the number of repetitions you perform the circuit to 10 by the end of the summer.

- Aquatic Circuit: (This workout is optional, since you may not have access to a pool.)
  ✓ Part #1 – waist-deep water:
    - jog two minutes
    - tuck jumps – 10 times
    - high knees
    - skipping
    - frog jumps – 10 times
    - backwards jog
  ✓ Part #2 – shoulder-deep water:
    - back to wall – arms extended, holding on to side – kick for one minute without breaking the water
    - back to wall – arms extended, holding on to side – kick for one minute – break water
    - face wall – hold on to side – kick for one minute – without breaking the water
    - face wall – hold on to side – kick for one minute – break water
  ✓ Part #3 – deep water:
    - tread water using your legs only, while keeping your hands out of the water–five minutes
    - tread water using your arms only – five minutes

✓ Part #4 – shoulder-deep water:

- arms extended out to the side – pull arms down to legs 10 times
- arms at legs – pull up out of the water 10 times
- arms extended out in front – pull down to sides of the body 10 times
- arms at side of your body – pull up out of the water 10 times
- hold on to side of pool for balance – start with legs together – pull one leg up in front 10 times
- start with one leg extended in front of your body – pull down 10 times (work both legs)

❑ **Training log**

Mark only those items you completed. You may also choose to lift two days a week.

- Week #1–(Refer to Figure 11.7)
- Week #2–(Refer to Figure 11.8)
- Week #3–(Refer to Figure 11.9)
- Week #4–(Refer to Figure 11.10)
- Week #5–(Refer to Figure 11.11)
- Week #6–Max out on core lifts (Refer to Figure 11.12)
- Week #7–(Refer to Figure 11.13)
- Week #8–(Refer to Figure 11.14)
- Week #9–(Refer to Figure 11.15)
- Week #10–(Refer to Figure 11.1

Monday	Tuesday	Wednesday	Thursday	Friday
❑ jump rope ❑ shooting ❑ 10-min. run ❑ weights (10, 8, 6, 4, 2)	❑ abdominals ❑ 1-mile run ❑ weights (10, 8, 6, 4, 2)	❑ jump rope ❑ shooting ❑ 10-min. run ❑ aquatics	❑ abdominals ❑ 1-mile run ❑ weights (10, 8, 6, 4, 2)	❑ jump rope ❑ shooting ❑ 10-min. run ❑ weights (10, 8, 6, 4, 2)

Figure 11.7. Week #1.

Monday	Tuesday	Wednesday	Thursday	Friday
❑ jump rope ❑ shooting ❑ 12-min. run ❑ weights (10, 8, 6, 4, 2)	❑ abdominals ❑ 1-mile run ❑ weights (10, 8, 6, 4, 2)	❑ jump rope ❑ shooting ❑ 12-min. run ❑ aquatics	❑ abdominals ❑ 1-mile run ❑ weights (10, 8, 6, 4, 2)	❑ jump rope ❑ shooting ❑ 12-min. run ❑ weights (10, 8, 6, 4, 2)

Figure 11.8. Week #2.

Monday	Tuesday	Wednesday	Thursday	Friday
❑ jump rope ❑ shooting ❑ 14-min. run ❑ weights (10, 8, 6, 4, 2)	❑ abdominals ❑ 1.5-mile run ❑ weights (10, 8, 6, 4, 2)	❑ plyometrics ❑ shooting ❑ 14-min. run ❑ aquatics	❑ abdominals ❑ 1.5-mile run ❑ weights (10, 8, 6, 4, 2)	❑ jump rope ❑ shooting ❑ 14-min. run ❑ weights (10, 8, 6, 4, 2)

Figure 11.9. Week #3.

Monday	Tuesday	Wednesday	Thursday	Friday
❑ jump rope ❑ shooting ❑ 16-min. run ❑ weights (10, 8, 6, 4, 2)	❑ abdominals ❑ 1.5-mile run ❑ weights (10, 8, 6, 4, 2)	❑ plyometrics ❑ shooting ❑ 16-min. run ❑ aquatics	❑ abdominals ❑ 1.5-mile run ❑ weights (10, 8, 6, 4, 2)	❑ jump rope ❑ shooting ❑ 16-min. run ❑ weights (10, 8, 6, 4, 2)

Figure 11.10. Week #4.

Monday	Tuesday	Wednesday	Thursday	Friday
❑ plyometrics ❑ shooting ❑ 18-min. run ❑ weights three sets of 10	❑ abdominals ❑ 2-mile run ❑ weights three sets of 10	❑ jump rope ❑ shooting ❑ 18-min. run ❑ aquatics	❑ abdominals ❑ 2-mile run ❑ weights three sets of 10	❑ plyometrics ❑ shooting ❑ 18-min. run ❑ weights three sets of 10

Figure 11.11. Week #5.

Monday	Tuesday	Wednesday	Thursday	Friday
❑ plyometrics ❑ shooting ❑ 20-min. run	❑ abdominals ❑ 2-mile run ❑ aquatics	❑ jump rope ❑ shooting ❑ 20-min. run ❑ max out	❑ abdominals ❑ 2-mile run ❑ aquatics	❑ plyometrics ❑ shooting ❑ 20-min. run

Bench:_____ Squat:_____ Hang clean:_____ Dead Lift:_____

Figure 11.12. Week #6.

Monday	Tuesday	Wednesday	Thursday	Friday
❑ jump rope ❑ shooting ❑ 6 x 200m in 35 sec with 90 sec rest ❑ weights (10, 8, 6, 4, 2)	❑ bleachers ❑ shooting ❑ weights (10, 8, 6, 4, 2)	❑ abdominals ❑ shooting ❑ 2-mile run ❑ aquatics	❑ bleachers ❑ shooting ❑ weights (10, 8, 6, 4, 2)	❑ jump rope ❑ shooting ❑ 6 x 200m in 35 sec with 90 sec rest ❑ weights (10, 8, 6, 4, 2)

Figure 11.13. Week #7.

Monday	Tuesday	Wednesday	Thursday	Friday
❑ jump rope ❑ shooting ❑ 6 x 200m in 35" with 90" rest ❑ weights (10, 8, 6, 4, 2)	❑ bleachers ❑ shooting ❑ weights (10, 8, 6, 4, 2)	❑ abdominals ❑ shooting ❑ 2-mile run ❑ aquatics	❑ bleachers ❑ shooting ❑ weights (10, 8, 6, 4, 2)	❑ jump rope ❑ shooting ❑ 6 x 200m in 35" with 90" rest ❑ weights (10, 8, 6, 4, 2)

Figure 11.14. Week #8.

Monday	Tuesday	Wednesday	Thursday	Friday
❑ jump rope ❑ shooting ❑ 6 x 100m 5 x 30m sprints ❑ weights (10, 8, 6, 4, 2)	❑ bleachers ❑ shooting ❑ 20-min. run ❑ weights (10, 8, 6, 4, 2)	❑ abdominals ❑ shooting ❑ 8 x 100m 5 x 75m sprints	❑ bleachers ❑ shooting ❑ 20-min. run ❑ weights (10, 8, 6, 4, 2)	❑ jump rope ❑ shooting ❑ 6 x 100m 5 x 30m sprints ❑ weights (10, 8, 6, 4, 2)

Figure 11.15. Week #9.

Monday	Tuesday	Wednesday	Thursday	Friday
❑ jump rope ❑ shooting ❑ 6 x 100m 5 x 30m sprints ❑ weights (3 x 10)	❑ bleachers ❑ shooting ❑ 20-min. run ❑ weights (3 x 10)	❑ abdominals ❑ shooting ❑ 8 x 100m 5 x 75m sprints	❑ bleachers ❑ shooting ❑ 20-min. run ❑ weights (3 x 10)	❑ jump rope ❑ shooting ❑ 6 x 100m 5 x 30m sprints ❑ weights (3 x 10)

Figure 11.16. Week #10.

Planning a Tournament

THREE TO FOUR MONTHS BEFORE THE TOURNAMENT:

❑ Send letter to prospective teams.

If your tournament is yearly, then you will probably already have a few teams that are "regulars." For your open spots, get the coaching directory out and start addressing letters. Some schools may have already committed to a tournament at the end of last year's season, but it doesn't hurt to try and recruit them for the next year. Figure A-1 illustrates an example of a letter I sent one year to over 20 schools.

Dear Coach,

We would like to personally invite you to participate in our 47th Annual Toucan Basketball Tournament. The tournament will be limited to eight teams in the 2A or 3A classification only.

The dates for the tournament are December 9, 10, and 11. We will award the following:

- *First-place trophy*
- *Second-place trophy*
- *Third-place trophy*
- *Consolation trophy*

- *Trophies to championship team members*
- *10 All-Tournament trophies*
- *One MVP trophy*
- *One plaque for the outstanding coach*

We will also have a free-throw contest, a three-point contest, concessions for the players, and a hospitality room for the coaches. The tournament fee is $100 per team. I'm looking forward to hearing from you if you would like to participate. Enclosed is a response card. Please fill it out and return it to me by October 15. If I can help you in any way, please contact me at school (555-111-1212) or at home (999-123-1212).

Figure A.1. Sample recruitment letter.

You might want to include a self-addressed stamped envelope for the response cards. Figure A.2. illustrates an example of a response card.

```
School Name: _____

❑ Would like to participate in the tournament.

❑ Will not participate this year.

❑ Interested in participating next year.

Please return no later than October 15th.
Thanks.
```

Figure A.2. Sample response card.

SIX WEEKS BEFORE THE TOURNAMENT:

❑ Send another letter confirming participation in tournament with list of teams entered, an information sheet for the program, and a bracket. Figure A.3-A.5 illustrate an example of a confirmation letter, an information sheet, and a tournament bracket, respectively.

Dear Coach,

Welcome to the 47th Annual Toucan Basketball Tournament. We are looking forward to having you visit Taylor. The following teams are entered:

Bellview	AA	Hallsville	A
Banterville	AAA	Montgomery	AAA
Beantown	AA	Rocktown	AA
Flounderville	AAA	Taylor	AA

Enclosed is an information sheet and a tournament bracket. The top team is the home team and will wear white. Please fill out the information sheet and return it to me by November 18. You may fax it to: 911-800-1212.

We will stay on a tight schedule, allowing eight minutes between games, with a five-minute halftime intermission. We will also provide warm-up balls.

Good luck this season and contact me if you have any questions.

Figure A.3. A sample confirmation letter.

```
                    Taylor Toucan Tournament
                        Information Sheet


School Name: _____ Coach: _____

School Colors: _____ Dist/Class: _____

No.    Name                    Position        Class           Ht.

___    _____         _____      _____      ___

___    _____         _____      _____      ___

___    _____         _____      _____      ___

___    _____         _____      _____      ___

___    _____         _____      _____      ___

___    _____         _____      _____      ___

___    _____         _____      _____      ___

___    _____         _____      _____      ___

___    _____         _____      _____      ___

___    _____         _____      _____      ___

___    _____         _____      _____      ___
```

Figure A.4. A sample information sheet.

Tournament Brackets

At a minimum, try to get at least eight teams to participate in the tournament and construct a bracket similar to the one illustrated in Figure A.5. Figure A.5 shows the standard bracket most people use for an eight-team tournament. It can even be used with seven teams, with one team getting a bye. Fortunately, if you need assistance in constructing a bracket for a tournament with an unusual number of teams, plenty of tools (books, Cd-ROM programs, etc.) are available on the market. Another possibility would be to conduct the tournament using a round-robin type format. This format could be used for a much smaller tournament (six teams or less). Figure A.6 illustrates an example of a four-team tournament in a round-robin format:

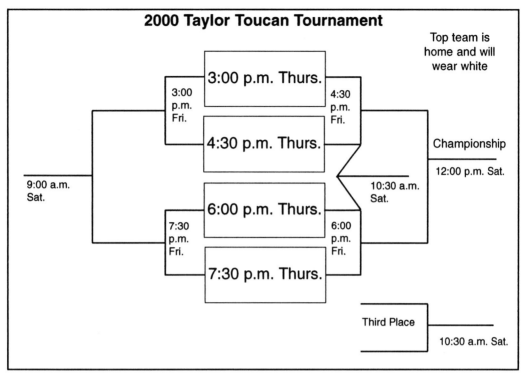

Figure A.5. A sample tournament bracket for eight teams.

Thursday, Dec. 10	Friday, Dec. 11	Saturday, Dec. 12
Welch vs. Mt. Ida	Gilmer vs. Mt. Ida	Welch vs. Gilmer
3:30 Women	3:30 Women	3:30 Women
5:00 Men	5:00 Men	5:00 Men
Taylor vs. Gilmer	Taylor vs. Welch	Taylor vs. Mt. Ida
6:30 Women	6:30 Women	6:30 Women
8:00 Men	8:00 Men	8:00 Men

Note: The winner is determined by overall record, team-to-team competition, and point-spread carryover up to 12 points.

Figure A.6. A sample round-robin bracket for four schools.

ONE MONTH BEFORE THE TOURNAMENT

❏ Make sure you have officials scheduled.

❏ Assign coaches to run the clock and monitor the scoreboard for all games.

❏ Order trophies and plaques.

❏ Order or make programs.

❏ Find a gatekeeper.

• *SCHEDULING OFFICIALS*

It would be wise to schedule at least four officials for each day of the tournament. Then, each set of two officials could alternate working games. After watching them on Thursday and Friday, you could then choose your best two officials for the championship game on Saturday.

• *ASSIGNING THE CLOCK AND BOOK*

This might be the biggest headache you encounter in planning your tournament. You could go and ask each coach if they'd be willing to work for three days, and you might get one to agree, depending on the staff. It's much easier if your athletic director backs you and assigns coaches to do the job. Otherwise, you'll have to find parents to help, and they usually aren't knowledgeable enough about the game to keep either the scorebook or the clock (especially). Figure A.7 illustrates an example of a completed tournament assignment schedule.

ASSIGNMENTS FOR TOURNAMENT				
December 8, Thursday				
3:00 p.m.	Clock:	Jon W.	Book:	Tammy M.
4:30 p.m.	Clock:	Jon W.	Book:	Tammy M.
6:00 p.m.	Clock:	Scott K.	Book:	Tammy M.
7:30 p.m.	Clock:	Stephenie	Book:	Tammy M.
December 9, Friday				
3:00 p.m.	Clock:	Susan B	Book:	Tammy M.
4:30 p.m.	Clock:	Pritchett	Book:	Susan B..
6:00 p.m.	Clock:	Ron P..	Book:	Jackie S.
7:30 p.m.	Clock:	Ron P.	Book:	Jackie S.

Figure A.7. A sample tournament assignment schedule.

- *ORDERING AWARDS*

There may be a company your athletic director prefers that you use, so be sure to ask him. You will need to order the following:

- ✓ First-place team trophy
- ✓ Second-place team trophy
- ✓ Third-place team trophy
- ✓ Consolation trophy
- ✓ Individual trophies for the champions (optional)
- ✓ All-Tournament trophies (however many you decide is appropriate – eight to 10 is plenty)
- ✓ MVP award
- ✓ Three-point award
- ✓ Free-throw award
- ✓ Outstanding-coach award

- *GETTING THE PROGRAMS READY*

You can either have the programs printed by an outside company or do them yourself. With the scanners and computers that are currently available, you can make a pretty nice program yourself. If you want to save some money, do it yourself. It doesn't have to be elaborate. Most people just want to see their kid's name and number in print. Among the factors involving your programs that you need to address are the following:

✓ *Decide on a cover.* Figure A.8 illustrates an example of a sample program cover that could be used. Nothing very fancy, but it works.

Figure A.8. Sample program cover.

✓ *Type an appreciation to go on the inside cover.* It could say something similar to the example shown in Figure A.9.

> *The Lady Toucans take this opportunity to express our appreciation to the many people who help make our tournament possible. Our sincere appreciation and thanks to the following members of the athletic department: Stan Labay, Athletic Director; Coaches Jon Wunderlick, Tammy Massengale, Scott Kana, Archie Seals, Susan Brewer and Reggie Crawford, for their time and effort in making this a successful tournament.*
>
> *In this, our 47th annual tournament, we wish to welcome the following teams, coaches, managers and fans to Taylor High School: Brazos, Montgomery, Hempstead, RTC, Boling, and Rockdale.*
>
> *Warm-up basketballs will be furnished by Taylor I.S.D. Eight minutes will be allowed for pre-game warm-up and a five-minute, half-time intermission. Admission price will be $2.00 for adults and $1.00 for students per session. A coaches' lounge with refreshments will be provided. We ask the teams and fans not to take food or drinks into the gymnasium. Thank you for your consideration of our building and facilities, and we hope you enjoy the tournament.*

Figure A.9. Sample appreciation remarks.

✓ *Locate and type out any records from previous tournaments.* You might try to find former tournament champions and the scores and tournament records. If you don't have any of that information because it is the first year for the tournament, be sure to keep records for the next year. The following are some examples of records to keep:

• Individual high score for one game	52, Ann Moon, Angleton, 1977
• Individual free throws for one game	33, Marie Wolle, RTC, 1969
• Individual high score for series	178 (4 games), A. Moon, Angleton, 1977
• Aggregate high score one game	146 (Waller 76, Bellville 70), 1974
• Aggregate low score one game	30 (Carmine 24, Bellville 'B' 6), 1949
• Team high score one game	89, RTC, 1970
• Team low score one game	5, Bellville 'B', 1949
• Team high score for series	296 (4 games), Bellville, 1976

✓ *Include the tournament results from the previous year on another page.* Figure A10. illustrates an example of such an entry.

✓ *Get all of the information sheets from each coach and get them typed.* If one team doesn't send you the information sheet back, call them and have them fax you one. If they don't get you one on time, they just miss out. As a general rule, allow one page per team. In fact, you can combine several teams on one sheet if you are short on paper or funds. Figure A.11 illustrates a sample information sheet.

1993 TOURNAMENT RESULTS

Championship Game: Tomball 84, Taylor 30
Third Place: Montgomery 46, Giddings 51
Consolation: Sealy 54, Hempstead 46

ALL TOURNAMENT TEAM

Most Valuable Player: Rochelle Larabee, Tomball
Winning Coach: Karen Lemker

Tiffany Schmidt, Taylor	Lana Laskoskie, Taylor
Kelli Schrader, Taylor	S. Mayo, Brazos
B. Brown, Brazos	Belinda Brooks, Hempstead
Shanna Reed, Waller	Melissa Page, Tomball
Tashawana Johnston, Tomball	Bethie Younger, Tomball

Figure A.10. Sample prior tournament results page.

Rockdale Tigerettes

No.	Name	Class	Ht.
10	Karla Hurd	Junior	5'11
12	Casey Johnston	Senior	5'8
14	Sharon Wallis	Junior	5'5
20	Brandie Baker	Soph.	5'9
22	Stacie Rash	Soph.	5'10
24	Courtney Kellar	Junior	5'5
32	Cadie Stork	Soph.	5'6
44	Krista Robinson	Senior	5'11

Head Coach: Janet Havelka
Assistants: Mickey Rundell, Laura Boyer
Manager: Beth Burnett

Figure A.11. A sample completed information sheet.

✓ *Take a copy of the tournament bracket and reduce it to fit in the program.*

✓ *Now all you have to do is run it off!* Make the program with legal-size paper (8.5" x 14"). Cut and paste your copies onto the legal-size sheets. You will need eight sheets to begin. Figure A.12 illustrates a sample 8-sheet, program layout.

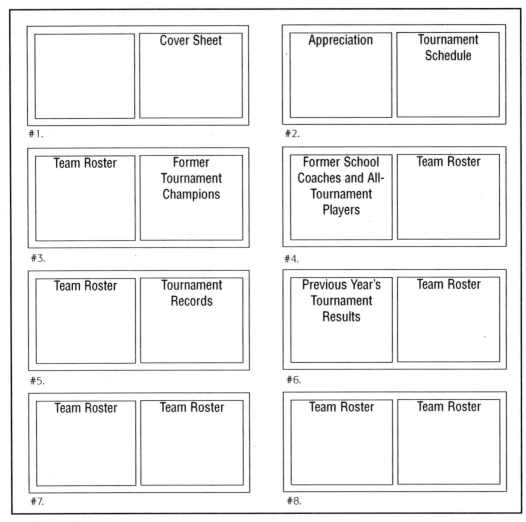

Figure A.12. Sample eight-sheet, program layout.

Page two should be copied onto the back of page one. Page four should be copied onto the back of page three and so on. Once you have made your two-sided copies, you then place page seven/eight on top of page five/six and so on. You then fold the pages in half, and you have your program. If you have a heavy-duty stapler, you can staple in the fold to help keep it all together. If this is your first year to run a tournament or you don't have records of previous tournaments, Figure A.13 illustrates a basic program outline.

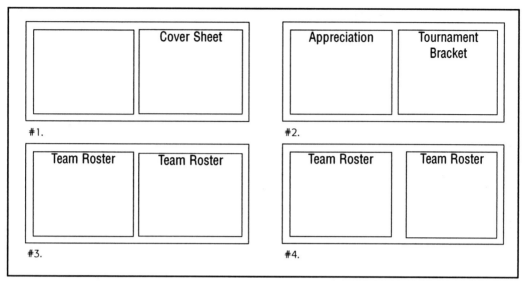

Figure A.13. Basic four-sheet program outline.

- *FINDING A GATEKEEPER*

Your school may have someone who usually keeps the gate for the regular season basketball games. If you don't have a regular gatekeeper, or that person isn't willing to sit for that long, then add that responsibility to your clock and book assignment list.

TWO WEEKS BEFORE THE TOURNAMENT

❑ Have all your athletes sign up to bring something for the hospitality room.

- *HOSPITALITY ROOM FOOD*

The coaches who attend your tournament are usually impressed by two factors: keeping on schedule and what kind of food you have in the hospitality room. Have your athletes sign up to bring something, and then check it to make sure there aren't too many desserts vs. real food, etc. You will probably want to purchase cups and canned drinks (using tournament-fee money).

ONE WEEK BEFORE THE TOURNAMENT

❑ Make a large bracket sign to post on the wall.

❑ Make signs with team names to post on the wall.

❑ Make packets for the coach of each team.

❑ Get large envelopes for the packets.

❑ Order hors d'oeuvres tray for hospitality room.

❑ Send information to the local paper.

- *SIGNS WITH TEAM NAMES*

These signs will be used to designate the home team and the visiting team for the fans. Post them under the clock on the wall.

- **PACKETS FOR COACHES**

The packets for each coach should include the following:

- A letter to the coach (Refer to Figure A.14)

- A free-throw and three-point shooting sign-up sheet

- Three All-Tournament ballots (Refer to Figure A.17)

- A tournament bracket for the coach

- Programs for players and coaches

Welcome to the _____ Tournament. We hope that you enjoy the tournament and will return next year.

Enclosed you will find the following items:

> *Free throw and three-point sign-up sheet*

> *All-Tournament ballots (three)*

> *Bracket*

> *Programs for players and coaches*

Please fill out the free-throw and three-point shooting entry sheet immediately and return it to Stephenie Jordan. We will begin the free-throw competition on Thursday before each game and the three-point contest before each game on Friday. Each competitor will shoot 10 free throws. The three-point contest will be timed – the most made in one minute. At the completion of each game, please fill out the All-Tournament selection ballot and give it to Stephenie Jordan. Don't forget the coaches/officials hospitality room located in the coaches office. If you need anything, please let me know.

Figure A.14. A sample packet letter to the coach.

- *FREE-THROW AND THREE-POINT SHOOTING CONTEST SIGN-UP SHEET*

The point of having the sign-up sheet is to make sure you have the correct names of the participants. Once you have all of the names, transfer them to a master sheet where you can record the results. This step will make it easier for you to determine the winner. See Figures A.15 and A.16.

- *INFORMATION TO NEWSPAPER*

Send your local newspaper any pre-tournament information that can be printed for a story (e.g. favored team, outstanding players, outstanding coaches or any other tidbits of information). A finalized tournament schedule should also be included.

Please print the names of your Free Throw and Three-Point participants in the blanks provided:

FREE THROW: _____

THREE-POINT: _____

The participants will compete five minutes prior to the game.

Free-Throw contest: Best out of 10 shots

Three-Point contest: Most made in one minute.

Winners will be announced at the completion of the championship game.

Figure A.15. A sample sign-up sheet for the free-throw and three-point shooting contest.

FREE THROW PARTICIPANTS

Team	Name	Number
Taylor Varsity	_____	_____
Taylor J.V.	_____	_____
Boling	_____	_____
Brazos	_____	_____
Hempstead	_____	_____
Montgomery	_____	_____
Rockdale	_____	_____

Figure A.16. A sample master results sheet.

47th Annual Brahmanette Tournament
All-Tournament Ballot

Nominate two players from your team and two players from the opponent's team. Indicate your nominees by each player's number.

Nominating coach: _____

Name of your team: _____ Opponent's team: _____

1. _____   1. _____

2. _____   2. _____

Figure A.17. A sample all-tournament ballot.

THE DAY BEFORE THE TOURNAMENT

- ❏ Remind all athletes to bring food for the hospitality room.
- ❏ Buy cups, napkins, utensils, plates, and canned drinks.
- ❏ Prepare the ice chests.
- ❏ Put reminders in the coaches' boxes listing the times they work.
- ❏ Make an excuse list for your team if they play before school is out.
- ❏ Prepare the score book to be used as the official book.
- ❏ Pick up the hor d'oeuvres tray.
- ❏ Set up the gym (chairs, scorer's table, bleachers out).

THE FIRST DAY OF THE TOURNAMENT (THURSDAY)

- ❏ Make coffee for the hospitality room.
- ❏ Get ice and cover drinks in coolers.
- ❏ Make sure dressing rooms are clean.
- ❏ Set up hospitality room as athletes bring food.
- ❏ Give programs to the gatekeeper.
- ❏ Give coaches information packets as they arrive and direct them to the dressing rooms.

- ❑ Have pencils ready for the score book.
- ❑ Set up the clock.
- ❑ Have a rack of balls ready for pre-game warm-ups.

Once the games begin, the hard part is over! After each day, be sure the dressing rooms are clean and the food is put up.

THE SECOND DAY OF THE TOURNAMENT (FRIDAY)

The set-up is the same as for Thursday. If you have a team that will not be returning on Saturday for any of the trophy games, be sure to give the coach any all-tournament trophies her player's might have received. As such, you'll have to tabulate some votes fairly quickly on Friday. Chances are they won't have many players on an all-tournament team, or if they do, they'll be an obvious choice.

THE LAST DAY OF THE TOURNAMENT (SATURDAY)

After each trophy game, just hand the coach her team's trophy and get ready for the next game. It doesn't have to be a big production unless you want it to be. All-tournament selections should be announced at the conclusion of the championship game.

AFTER THE TOURNAMENT

- ❑ Call in tournament results to newspaper.
- ❑ Send a letter to participating coaches.
- ❑ Send a thank you to your helpers.

- *RESULTS*

Fax or call in the tournament results to your local paper as soon as the tournament ends. You might want to include the three-point and free throw shooting contest champions, as well as the MVP, tournament champions, etc. The sportswriter will ask you what he wants to include in the results.

- *LETTER TO COACHES*

Send a letter to each coach who participated in the tournament and include the final results of the tournament. Figure A.18 illustrates an example of a letter that could be sent to each coach.

> *Dear Coach,*
>
> *We hope you enjoyed the 47th Annual Toucan Basketball Tournament and hope you will plan to participate in the tournament next year. We have had interest from other 2A and 3A schools which will make this event even more exciting and competitive.*
>
> *Enclosed are the tournament results. The Taylor coaching staff hopes you are successful this season and look forward to hearing from you in the spring when we begin planning next year's tournament.*

Figure A.18. A sample coaches' letter.

• *LETTER TO HELPERS*

You should jot a note to all those who helped keep the book, gate, etc. Figure A.19 shows an example of a letter of appreciation that could be sent to those individuals who helped you run the tournament.

> *To:*
>
> *From: Coach Jordan*
>
> *The Lady Toucan Basketball Team and I would like to express our appreciation to you for your help and support during the tournament. Your efforts were a big part of making our tournament a success.*

Figure A.19. A sample helper's letter.

Organizing a Youth Program

THE FORMAT

Use high school student-athletes as coaches for each team in the program. The participants enjoy working with high school basketball players and the student-athletes get to see the game from a different perspective. Run the program for five consecutive Saturdays, with the first Saturday designated as a skills day and draft day. The next four Saturdays are reserved for games and practices.

The chapter is presented in a timeline format to give you a clear picture of when and how to get started. Note: This program is based on the use of two gyms. You'll have to make adjustments if you only have one gym.

TIMELINE

- *EIGHT WEEKS BEFORE THE START OF THE PROGRAM:*
- ❏ Order (or borrow) any equipment you don't already have. If you've never had a youth program at your school, call other schools and borrow any equipment you need (if they're willing). The following are items that you might need to order:
  - ✓ Two small goals for first and second graders (should hook over normal goals and be eight feet from the floor)
  - ✓ 10-12 junior-size basketballs

✓ Six sets of nylon pinnies with numbers

✓ Colored wristbands (white, red, navy, purple, green) – four of each color

- *SIX WEEKS BEFORE THE START OF THE PROGRAM:*
  - ❑ Find some basketball officials that will either work for free or for about five dollars a game. Consider using former players who need the money or want to help out. You should have two officials for each game but you can get by with one (especially for the first and second graders). Find some people who will be *reliable*; otherwise you will be officiating the games.

- *FOUR WEEKS BEFORE THE START OF THE PROGRAM:*
  - ❑ Send a letter home with all elementary students addressed to parents. Include a registration form and insurance waiver. A sample letter is illustrated in Figure B.1.
  - ❑ Decide the dates for registration. (Have a registration form available at two home basketball games.) Refer the sample in Figure B.2.

- *TWO WEEKS BEFORE THE START OF THE PROGRAM:*
  - ❑ Have registration form for all age groups available at home basketball games.
  - ❑ Get a general number of how many students will participate in each division and determine how many teams you'll have.
  - ❑ Deposit money in either a school account or open an account at your local bank.
  - ❑ Call sporting goods stores or T-shirt printers to determine the best price for the t-shirts.
  - ❑ Determine where to order trophies.
  - ❑ Recruit high school athletes to be coaches.

Registration

Be sure to have the following items at the registration table:

✓ money box

✓ additional registration forms

✓ pens

✓ six manila envelopes (labeled: first- and second-grade boys, first- and second-grade girls, etc.)

Parents,

Very soon, we will be beginning the youth program for first- through-sixth graders. It will be coordinated a little differently than in the past. We will only meet on Saturdays, with no additional practices during the week. Boys' and girls' high school basketball players will do all coaching. High school coaches will be supervising all activities.

The first Saturday meeting will be on January 31st with a general skills introduction for all age groups with first and second graders meeting from 9:00-11:00 a.m., third and fourth graders from 12:00-2:00 p.m. and fifth and sixth graders from 3:00-5:00 p.m. We will adhere to this time schedule for all five Saturdays.

Teams will be drafted the afternoon of the first Saturday, and games will begin Saturday, Feb. 7th. A list of each team and its members will be posted on the Monday following the first session.

Registration fees and times are included on the registration form. Please fill out the appropriate information on the form, sign the insurance waiver, and bring your check to registration. Late registration will be on Saturday, January 31st from 8:00-8:30 a.m. No one will be admitted to the program after this time. Siblings will be offered a family rate.

Each child will receive a trophy for participating in the program and a T-shirt to be worn during each Saturday session.

IMPORTANT NOTE: We ask that you not leave your children at the gym without your supervision.

If you have any questions, please contact me at 555-1212.

Sincerely,

Coach Jordan

Figure B.1. Sample letter to parents of youth program participants.

Finding a good deal on T-shirts

I have a local printer who I use who charges me $4.25 a shirt and will take a purchase order from the school.

YOUTH BASKETBALL REGISTRATION FORM

Please fill out the following information and return, with your registration fee, to Stephenie Jordan on the following dates:

- January 15th or January 22nd from 4:00 – 8:00 p.m. in the main foyer of the gym.

- Late registration will be from 8:00-8:30 a.m. on January 31st. There will be an additional charge $5 per child.

The registration fees are as follows:

$25 per child

$40 for two siblings

$60 for three siblings

Make checks payable to: Your school name or organization

Name of child: _____ Boy: ❑ Girl: ❑

Check appropriate age category: ❑ First and second grade

❑ Third and fourth grade

❑ Fifth and sixth grade

Circle T-shirt size: YS YM YL AS AM AL AXL

Read carefully and sign the following insurance waiver:

I hereby give my consent for the above child to compete in the Youth Program. It is understood that although there is appropriate supervision, the possibility of accident still remains. Neither the high school, coaches, nor other personnel assumes any responsibility in case an accident occurs. If, in the judgment of any representative of Youth Basketball, the above child needs immediate care, and treatment as a result of an injury or sickness, I hereby request, authorize and consent to such care and treatment as may be given to said child by any physician, trainer, nurse, or Youth Basketball representative. I do hereby agree to not sue and to release, indemnify, and hold harmless, the Garrison I.S.D., its affiliates, officers, directors, volunteers, and employees from any and all liability, claims, demands, and causes of action whatsoever, arising out of my child's participation in this event and related activities.

I have read, understand, and agree to the terms of this Agreement.

Date: _____

Signature of parent or guardian: _____

Printed name of parent or guardian: _____

Figure B.2. Youth program registration form.

Finding the right trophies

I usually spend about $5 - $7 on each trophy, but you can get them as inexpensively as $3.50 each. Give a first place trophy to all members of the team that wins the division and give everyone else a participation trophy, so each child goes home with one trophy.

Recruiting coaches

Have your students sign up during their athletic periods. They need to put their age preference, who they would like to coach with, and their T-shirt size (each student-coach has the option to purchase a T-shirt with the Little Dribbler's emblem and "Coach" on the front). After registration, accommodate the requests of your basketball players regarding their age preference. You should have at least two coaches per team, but you can add a third if necessary.

- *ONE WEEK BEFORE THE START OF THE PROGRAM:*

  ❑ Meet with the student-coaches.

  ❑ Call pizza places to sponsor the youth program.

Coaches Meeting

At the coaches meeting, you will need to stress the importance of attendance on all five Saturdays. Give them a packet with the following information: (Note: Keep in mind that you don't want to give them too much, or they may lose it before they need it.)

✓ introductory letter
✓ coaching assignments
✓ schedule for first Saturday
✓ rules of the game
✓ station assignments
✓ rules to teach at stations
✓ teaching progression for stations
✓ substitution pattern for games
✓ sample practice schedule

Introductory Letter

You should send a letter to each of your coaches to outline the basic parameters of the youth program and what you expect from each coach. You will need to cover each revelant point in your letter to your boys' and girls' coaches. A sample letter is illustrated in Figure B.3.

Coach,

I am very glad you have decided to volunteer your time and knowledge for the Little Dribbler's program this year. It is a fun job with great responsibility. By signing up to coach, you are committing yourself to at least two hours a day for five Saturdays. The players you coach will be looking up to you and counting on you to be there every Saturday.

Here are just a few things to remember:

• During the introductory session, be sure you are keeping all of your kids involved in the activity. Don't slack off for even a minute.

• While coaching a game, you must adhere to the substitution list so that all students will get a chance to play. Any cheating will not be tolerated.

• Be on time. You are required to be there at least 15 minutes prior to your team's start time. Do not show up right as the session or game is starting.

• Do not bring food and sit on the bench to coach your team. Be active and coach!

• Payment for shirts is $1.00.

• Never use foul language in front of the kids and never yell at them during the course of the game. Always be positive and supportive, whether you like them or not!

• Make sure you watch all of the kids during the first session, so you know who you might want to draft. It's the kids who you might pick last who will make the difference on your team.

• Have your practices planned out beforehand. Don't make it up as you go, because there are parents watching!

Figure B.3. Sample introductory letter to your coaches.

Coaching Assignments

Print a list with each coach's name and age division.

Schedule for First Saturday

The first meeting is a general skills introduction for all age groups. The participants will be guided through six stations, where each coach will teach basic fundamentals and a set of rules of basketball (e.g., what is the call if you dribble with two hands?). The coaches will also have an opportunity to see every player and make note of who they would like to draft that afternoon. Each of the coaches will be given a schedule like the one illustrated in Figure B.4. Each of the items mentioned will be explained later in this section.

```
1st and 2nd Grade:

 9:00 – 9:10     Welcome and introductions of all coaches
 9:15 – 10:00    Stations (nine minutes each)
10:00 – 10:25    Full-court relays, two-line lay-ups
10:30 – 10:50    Knock-out
10:50 – 11:00    Closing remarks
 5:30 – 7:00     Return to school for pizza and drafting of teams


3rd and 4th Grade:

12:00 – 12:10    Welcome and introductions of all coaches
12:15 – 1:00     Stations
 1:00 – 1:25     Full-court relays, two-line lay-ups
 1:30 – 1:50     Knock-out
 1:50 – 2:00     Closing
 5:30 – 7:00     Return to school for pizza and drafting of teams


5th and 6th Grade:

 3:00 – 3:10     Welcome and introductions of all coaches
 3:15 – 4:00     Stations
 4:00 – 4:25     Full-court relay, two-line lay-ups
 4:30 – 4:50     Knock-out
 4:50 – 5:00     Closing
 5:30 – 7:00     Return to school for pizza and drafting of teams
```

Figure B.4. Sample schedule for the first Saturday of the youth program.

Rules of the Game

All games consist of Four six-minute quarters and a running clock. All participants are required to play an equal amount of time. The coach should substitute new players every three minutes. There is a specific substitution pattern that should be followed. Once possession of the ball has changed, your team must get back to half-court. There will be no full-court pressing for grades one through four, but will be allowed in the last two minutes of the game for the fifth and six graders. The first and second grade teams will play man-to-man defense using the armbands* to avoid any confusion. If there is more than one defender on a player, the team will be told to "find their man." Zone defense will be allowed in the older divisions and is recommended especially if a team is winning by a large margin. There are no three-point shots for first through fourth grades.

*Each team is issued five different colored armbands. While on the court, there should be one member of each opposing team wearing the same colored armband. This player is who they are to guard while they are playing. Armbands may not be switched once play has started, but may be switched during a time-out or substitution.

Station Assignments (Refer to Figure B.5)

The first Saturday session involves the following six stations:

- Dribbling drills
- Ball-handling drills
- Lay-up drills
- Free throws
- Passing drills
- Shooting drills

Assign at least two coaches for each station — preferably one boy and one girl. The participants will be assigned to a station and will go through the drills for eight minutes. When one minute remains in the drill period, the coaches should sit all the participants down and go over the set of rules assigned to their station. At the buzzer, all participants should huddle up with the coaches, "break it down," and go to the next station.

Station Assignments for January 31st:

Station #1:   Dribbling drills:

  - S1:   Crystal Soto, John Jackson

  - S2:   Desirae Baggett, John Jackson

  - S3:   Brent Kelley, Kenya Simon

Station #2:   Shooting drills:

  - S1:   Jessica Stokes, Ryan Davis

  - S2:   Kyle Adkison, Shelitra Shepherd•

  S3:   Cory Bell, Ryan Williamson, Jason Fletcher

... and so on.

S1, S2, S3 = Session 1, Session 2, Session 3

Figure B.5. Sample station assignments form.

Rules to Teach at Each Station

❑ Station #1:

  ✓ How is the game started? (A jump ball in the center of the court.)

  ✓ How many players can play on one team at a time? (Five.)

- ✓ Name two ways to move the ball down the floor. (Pass, dribble, roll, tip, throw.)
- ✓ When time runs out and the score is tied, what happens? (An extra period is played—common referred to as overtime).
- ✓ What is the length of a high school quarter? (Eight minutes.)

☐ Station #2:

- ✓ What are the out-of-bounds lines? (Baselines, sidelines.)
- ✓ How many seconds does a team have to get the ball across half-court? (10.)
- ✓ What is a three-second lane violation? (When an offensive player stands in the lane for three seconds while his/her team has the ball.)
- ✓ What is "double-dribble"? (Dribbling, catching the ball, then dribbling again or dribbling with two hands at the same time.)
- ✓ What is the foot called that must stay planted? (Pivot foot.)

☐ Station #3:

- ✓ If a player takes a charge, what happened and who gets the foul? (A defensive player has set his/her position and is knocked down by an offensive player – the offensive player is charged with the foul.)
- ✓ What is a back-court violation? (When an offensive team crosses half-court after establishing possession in the front court.)
- ✓ How many fouls disqualify a player from the game? (Five.)
- ✓ What kind of foul is given for unsportsmanlike conduct? (Technical.)
- ✓ Who shoots a technical foul and how many shots does he/she get? (Anyone the coach picks. Two.)

☐ Station #4:

- ✓ How many seconds does a player have to shoot a free throw once the official gives the shooter the ball? (Five.)
- ✓ Who occupies the first place on each side of the lane closest to the basket? (The opponent of the shooter.)
- ✓ Can a player on the lane distract the shooter by waving his/her arms? (No.)
- ✓ When can a player on the lane enter to rebound the ball? (When the ball leaves the shooter's hand.)
- ✓ When can the shooter cross the free-throw line and enter the lane? (When the ball hits the rim.)

❑ Station #5:

- ✓ What happens if a free throw doesn't touch anything? (The other team gets the ball if it's the last shot; otherwise, shoot the second free throw.)

- ✓ What is "holding"? (Grabbing an opponent.)

- ✓ How many fouls can a team have in a half before the opponents are in the bonus (get to shoot free throws)? (When the team commits their seventh foul, the opponents shoot one-and-one.)

- ✓ When does a team automatically shoot two free throws? (After 10 team fouls.)

- ✓ What happens if two players have possession of the ball at the same time? (Possession alternates after the first jump ball.)

❑ Station #6:

- ✓ How many time-outs can a team take? (Four.)

- ✓ When does the clock stop? (When the official blows the whistle.)

- ✓ When does the clock start when the ball is inbounded? (As soon as the ball is touched, the official brings his/her arm down to indicate when the clock should start.)

- ✓ How is each quarter started? (The ball is taken out of bounds and thrown in by the team who has the next jump ball possession.)

- ✓ What is a "carry"? (Using the hand to lift the ball from underneath instead of pushing on top.)

Teaching Progression for Stations

Provide each coach with a teaching progression for the skill they are to teach. They can certainly come up with drills of their own, but the following information can be used as a guideline of what should be taught.

❑ Shooting

Coaching Points:

- ✓ Stance – the shooting foot points toward the target and the shoulder and hips face the basket.

- ✓ Finger position – the hand should be open with the fingers spread out on the ball with the ball resting on fingertips.

✓ Arm position – place the shooting hand on the thigh and raise the arm straight up until the bicep is at a 45-degree angle.

✓ Follow through – the middle and index fingers should push through the ball with the fingers pointed down toward the floor and the wrist turned slightly outward.

Drills: Around the world; in and out shooting; baby jump shots; etc.

❑ Lay-ups

Coaching Points:

✓ Introduce the lay-up with a one-foot takeoff beginning with the last step on the takeoff foot (without the ball). Focus on bringing the opposite knee high and hopping toward the backboard. Add the ball only after the takeoff has been mastered.

✓ Line the players up at the free-throw line extended at a 45-degree angle. Without the ball, have the players walk through using a three-step approach.

✓ Add one dribble to the three-step approach. The ball hits the floor as the first step is taken. Shoot at the end of the approach.

Drills: Two-line lay-ups on both sides.

❑ Dribbling

Coaching Points:

✓ Teach the yo-yo-like movement of the forearm and hand in a stationary position. Make sure the players are using the pads of their fingers and not slapping at the ball. Add eye contact, protecting the ball, switching hands, and increasing the speed of the dribble.

Drills: Use dominant hand and walk to half-court line and back. Then use the non-dominant hand and walk to half-court line and back. Increase to a jog. Add cones.

❑ Passing

Coaching Points:

✓ Teach a chest pass, emphasizing the use of two hands and a follow-through.

✓ Make sure the fingers are pointed at the receiver, with the thumbs pointing down and the palms out after the pass.

✓ Teach players to receive a pass and pivot (protecting the ball as they pivot).

Drills: Partner passing from different distances: chest pass; bounce pass; overhead pass. Four man passing – emphasizing the pivot star drill (if age appropriate).

❑ Defense

Coaching Points:

✓ Get in a slightly bent-knee position with the feet shoulder-width apart. One foot should be slightly ahead of the other.

✓ The head should be up and the back should be straight.

✓ The weight should be on the balls of the feet.

✓ The arms should be out with the palms up.

✓ Teach players to force the offensive players to change directions or dribble with their weak hand.

Drills: Slides; Quick feet; 2-1-2 zone responsibilities.

❑ Ballhandling

Coaching Points: Stress the point that the kids need to work on these drills every day!

Drills: Around body – reverse; around each leg; around both legs with feet together; figure eight; quick hands; dominant-hand dribbling; non-dominant hand dribbling.

Substitution Pattern for Games

Each participant will be wearing a pinnie with a number on it. During the game, a total of seven substitutions will be made. Each substitution will take place with three minutes left in each quarter and at the beginning of each quarter. If parents complain that once their kids get "in a groove" they have to come out of the game, just tell them this is the fairest way for all participants to get to play and that the program is designed as a learning experience for their children and just for fun. With 10 players, have two "teams" and sub in and out as a group. If a team is short a player, bring someone up from a younger age group. Plenty of kids are usually hanging around the gym anyway. Figure B.6 illustrates several patterns of substitution.

Practice Schedule

Stress that all practice time should be very structured. Give the coaches a sample practice schedule to follow similar to the one illustrated in Figure B.7.

7 Players:		
	IN	OUT
1.	1,2,3,4,5	(6,7)
2.	6,7,1,2,3	(4,5)
3.	4,5,6,7,1	(2,3)
4.	2,3,4,5,6	(1,7)
5.	7,1,2,3,4	(5,6)
6.	5,6,7,1,2	(3,4)
7.	3,4,5,6,7	(1,2)
8.	1,2,3,4,5	(6,7)

8 Players:		
	IN	OUT
1.	1,2,3,4,5	(6,7,8)
2.	6,7,8,1,2	(3,4,5)
3.	3,4,5,6,7	(1,2,8)
4.	8,1,2,3,4	(5,6,7)
5.	5,6,7,8,1	(2,3,4)
6.	2,3,4,5,6	(1,7,8)
7.	7,8,1,2,3	(4,5,6)
8.	4,5,6,7,8	(1,2,3)

9 Players:		
	IN	OUT
1.	1,2,3,4,5	(6,7,8,9)
2.	6,7,8,9,1	(2,3,4,5)
3.	2,3,4,5,6	(1,7,8,9)
4.	7,8,9,1,2	(3,4,5,6)
5.	3,4,5,6,7	(1,2,8,9)
6.	8,9,1,2,3	(4,5,6,7)
7.	4,5,6,7,8	(1,2,3,9)
8.	9,1,2,3,4	(5,6,7,8)

Figure B.6. Possible substitution patterns.

5 – 10 minutes	Warm-up drill:	lay-ups, 3-man weave, full-court dribble
5 – 10 minutes	Individual skills:	post moves, ball-handling drills, passing, shooting
10 – 15 minutes	Team offense	
10 – 15 minutes	Team defense	
5 minutes	Free Throws	

Figure B.7. Sample practice schedule.

• THE DAY BEFORE THE START OF THE PROGRAM:

❑ Make sure all equipment is accessible.

❑ Meet with the coaches once more to stress attendance and being on time.

❑ Have a list of all participants printed for an attendance check.

❑ Have overhead transparencies of all lists for the draft.

List of participants

Include the participant's T-shirt size so you can sort them according to age groups when you get them. Figure B.8 illustrates an example of a participant's form. The "team" column is for use during the draft.

Saturday #1:

- ❑ Set up for late registration.
- ❑ Hang small goals.
- ❑ Sweep the gym floor.
- ❑ Have junior-size balls out for free shooting before session starts.
- ❑ Post a sign on the door to let everyone know when the gym will open.
- ❑ Set up the sound system.
- ❑ Make sure the side goals are down.
- ❑ Meet with all coaches one more time before the doors open.
- ❑ Set up the game clock.
- ❑ Have someone pick up the pizzas, drinks, cups, ice, and napkins at 4:00 p.m.

Girls First and Second Grade

No.	Name	Grade	T-Shirt	Team
1	Adkison, Jordan	1st	YM	
2	Bear, C.J.	1st	YM	
3	Bell, Sykeitha	1st	YM	
4	Burkhalter, Amber	1st	YM	
5	Calhoun, Amanda	1st	YL	
6	Daniels, Jamisha	1st	YL	
7	Johnson, Traniqua	2nd	YM	
8	Lunsford, Danni	2nd	AS	
9	Miller, Lydia	2nd	YL	
10	Reneau, Amy	2nd	YM	
11	Reneau, Janie	2nd	YM	
12	Ross, LaTorshia	2nd	YM	
13	Story, Tamara	2nd	YM	
14	Walker, Faith	2nd	YM	
15	(for late registration)			
16				

Figure B.8. A sample for for listing participants.

Late Registration

Don't forget extra forms and the roll sheets. Add those individuals who register late to the roll sheets and the transparencies.

Getting the gym ready

Delegate as much as possible so you can attend to other things. Stay at the registration table until 8:30 a.m., and then begin meeting with your coaches. Have a few kids show up at 8:00 a.m. with you to get everything ready.

Post a sign

Post a sign to let people know the gym will not open until 8:50 a.m.

SCHEDULE OF EVENTS

Once the program actually begins, a number of events will occur, including welcoming and introducing the coaches, station work, full-court relays, two-line layups, knock-outs, and closing remarks.

• WELCOME AND INTRODUCTIONS OF ALL COACHES (FIVE MINUTES)

When you open the doors, it will be chaotic. Be sure all of your coaches are on the floor supervising and playing with the kids. Set the game clock for 10 minutes, while the kids shoot. When the buzzer goes off, bring everyone to the center of the court for the welcome and introductions. Tell them you're glad they're there, that it's going to be fun, etc. Then, introduce all of your coaches.

Once you've made the introductions, send the coaches to their stations and begin sending kids their way. Just have all of the kids stand up and face you. Next, point to a kid and then point to a station and tell her to sprint as fast as she can to the coach at that station. An example of a drill-station layout is illustrated in Figure B.9.

• STATIONS (45 MINUTES)

When all the participants are at a station, set the clock for nine minutes and start it. Hit the buzzer with about one minute left so that the coaches can sit the participants down and discuss the rules. Again, once the final buzzer sounds, the coaches should get their kids together in a huddle and then send them to the next station. When the players are at their final station, go to each station and let the coaches know to keep their kids when the final buzzer sounds.

- FULL-COURT RELAY, TWO-LINE LAY-UPS (25 MINUTES)

While all the kids are at their final station, tell the coaches to walk their team to the baseline for the full-court relays. You can do whatever relays you want to, including: right-hand dribble there and back, right-hand dribble there/left-hand back, etc. When each participant is finished, have her sit down to determine a winner. Once you've exhausted all relay possibilities, split the players into two groups and run two-line lay-ups.

- KNOCK-OUT (20 MINUTES)

It will take you just about 20 minutes for the coaches to teach the younger divisions how to even play knock-out. Knock-out involves the following rules:

> All players line up single file behind the free-throw line . The first two players in line each have a ball. Player #1 shoots at the goal. As she does, player #2 begins shooting at the goal. If player #1 makes the basket, player #2 passes the ball to player #3 and goes to the end of the line. If player #2 makes the basket before player #1, player #1 is out. Play continues until only one player is left.

- CLOSING REMARKS (FIVE MINUTES)

Explain that you will post the teams on Monday at the school; tell them how glad you are that they came; send them home.

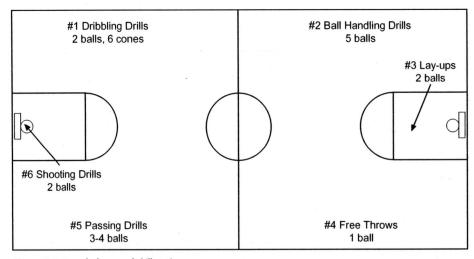

Figure B.9. Sample layout of drill stations.

- RETURN TO SCHOOL FOR PIZZA AND DRAFTING OF TEAMS (ONE HOUR).

Have your first- and second-grade coaches huddle around the overhead projector to start drafting their teams. The rest of the coaches can continue to eat pizza until it's their turn to draft. Determine who will have the first pick by drawing numbers out of a hat. Coaches will pick in order for the first round. The order of picks will change after each round. Have the coaches name their teams, and then begin the draft by letting whoever got number one choose their player. To be sure an even distribution of each grade exists in the teams, *pick all second graders first and then all the first graders*. An example of the drafting order is as follows:

	Round 1	Round 2	Round 3	Round 4
Team #1	first pick	fourth pick	third pick	second pick
Team #2	second pick	first pick	fourth pick	third pick
Team #3	third pick	second pick	first pick	fourth pick
Team #4	fourth pick	third pick	second pick	first pick

Note: The drafting order starts over again in round 5.

As the coaches choose their players, write the selections on the transparencies so everyone can see who has been picked and who is left.

Monday Before Saturday #2:

- ❑ Post teams on Monday.
- ❑ Call in T-shirt order and trophy order.
- ❑ Confirm officials.
- ❑ Get clock keepers and scorekeepers.
- ❑ Determine game schedule.

Recruiting Clock Keepers and Scorekeepers

The easiest way to recruit workers is to have a school club sponsor the program. Offer to split some of the earnings with them. A sample worker list is illustrated in Figure B.10.

T-shirts and Trophies

Have the T-shirts printed and ready for Saturday #2. Get help and sort all of the T-shirts according to when a team comes in. All you'll have to do is hand the pile of t-shirts to the coach and she can distribute them. Don't forget to order the coaches' shirts too. When you order the trophies, be sure to determine the number of players on the largest team, so you'll have enough first-place trophies regardless of which team wins.

Game schedule

The number of teams will obviously determine what kind of schedule you will have. Figure B.11 illustrates a wide variety of possible scheduling scenarios. Keep in mind that in order to play all the games and practice on the same day, the teams will practice for the first 30 minutes.

Date/Time	Clock Keeper	Scorekeeper
Feb. 7th		
9:00 a.m. (H.S.)		
12:00 p.m. (H.S.)		
12:00 p.m. (M.S.)		
3:00 p.m. (H.S.)		
3:00 p.m. (M.S.)		
Feb. 14th		
9:00 a.m. (H.S.)		
12:00 p.m. (H.S.)		
12:00 p.m. (M.S.)		
3:00 p.m. (H.S.)		
3:00 p.m. (M.S.)		
Feb. 21st		
9:00 a.m. (H.S.)		
12:00 p.m. (H.S.)		
12:00 p.m. (M.S.)		
3:00 p.m. (H.S.)		
3:00 p.m. (M.S.)		
Feb. 28th		
9:00 a.m. (H.S.)		
12:00 p.m. (H.S.)		
12:00 p.m. (M.S.)		
3:00 p.m. (H.S.)		
3:00 p.m. (M.S.)		

Figure B.10. A sample form for listing workers.

Key: 2G – 2B = two girls' teams and two boys' teams

2G – 2B (All games in main gym)

Game #1: G1 vs. G2

Game #2: B1 vs. B2

Because there will only be two games, extend the quarters to eight or 10 minutes and sub at four or five minutes. The schedule doesn't change.

2G – 3B (All games in main gym)

	Week 2	Week 3	Week 4	Week 5
Game #1:	B1 vs. B2	B2 vs. B3	B3 vs. B1	second place vs. third place
Game #2:	G1 vs. G2	G1 vs. G2	G1 vs. G2	G1 vs. G2
Game #3:	B1 vs. B3	B2 vs. B1	B3 vs. B2	first place vs. winner Game #1

3G – 3B

	Week 2	Week 3	Week 4	Week 5
Main gym				
Game #1:	B1 vs. B2	B2 vs. B3	B3 vs. B1	second place vs. third place
Game #2:	B1 vs. B3	B2 vs. B1	B3 vs. B2	first place vs. winner Game #1
Junior high gym				
Game #1:	G1 vs. G2	G2 vs. G3	G3 vs. G1	second place vs. third place
Game #2:	G1 vs. G3	G2 vs. G1	G3 vs. G2	first place vs. winner Game #1

3G – 4B

	Week 2	Week 3	Week 4	Week 5
Main gym				
Game #1:	B1 vs. B2	B2 vs. B3	B1 vs. B3	first place vs. fourth place
Game #2:	B3 vs. B4	B1 vs. B4	B2 vs. B4	second place vs. third place
Game #3:				winner Gm. #1 vs. winner Gm. #2
Junior high gym				
Game #1:	G1 vs. G2	G2 vs. G3	G3 vs. G1	second place vs. third place
Game #2:	G1 vs. G3	G2 vs. G1	G3 vs. G2	first place vs. winner Game #1

Figure B.11. A sample of possible scheduling options.

SCHEDULE OF EVENTS FOR NEXT THREE SATURDAYS

The gym should be open 10 minutes before the start time to practice for the kids to shoot around. When the buzzer sounds, all coaches should corral their players and begin practice. Practices will last 30 to 45 minutes, depending on the number of teams in each division. When you are setting your schedule with times, be sure to allow at least 40 to 45 minutes for each game. To speed things up, have all the teams practice in their pinnies so they are ready to go at game time. As soon as the last game of the session is over, collect all pinnies and reorganize them for the next age group. Then, clear the gym so you can regroup for the next session.

Saturdays #2, #3, and #4:

- ❑ Have the T-shirts ready for each coach to hand out (Saturday #2 only).
- ❑ Post the game schedule (with team names and specific times) on the wall for parents and friends to see.
- ❑ Get armbands for the first- and second-grade division.
- ❑ Get pinnies for all age groups.
- ❑ Provide whistles for the officials.
- ❑ Sweep the gym floor before each session.
- ❑ Get balls for practice and one or two game balls.
- ❑ Set up the game clock.

Saturday #5:

- ❑ Refer to the list from previous weeks.
- ❑ Have trophies sorted by age groups and ready to present immediately following each game.

Fund-Raising Ideas

If your program needs a few things, but there isn't enough money in the budget, you can generate up to $1000 per event by undertaking some of the following ideas. Keep in mind that while you can always resort to bake sales and car washes, these are much more fun.

POWDER PUFF FOOTBALL GAME

Powder puff is a flag-football game played by the girls on the Tuesday before the boys play your rival school. The game is played exactly like a regular Friday night game (officials, announcer, down markers, etc.) and is coached by varsity football players. We even have a pep rally that day with guy cheerleaders. If you can get your school's band to attend the game, it makes it an even better event. You need to get started by the first of September (or even sooner), if you want this idea to work.

How to Get Started

- ❏ Talk to your principal and get approval.
- ❏ Check with the football coach for use of the field.
- ❏ Have your principal call your rival's principal and get a name to contact.
- ❏ Put the date on the school calendar so it doesn't conflict with anything else.
- ❏ Have your school's varsity football players sign up to coach or be cheerleaders.

- ❑ Have girls sign up to play.
- ❑ Check with someone in the physical education department for football flags.
- ❑ Organize the concession stand.
- ❑ Arrange a time to meet with other potential sponsors.
- ❑ Talk to your cheerleading sponsor and/or cheerleaders.

- *Finding a sponsor*

The most difficult task may be finding someone from the other school to agree to sponsor such an event. After clearing this with your principal, you might ask that individual to call the principal from the other school and find out if they would be interested. If the other school's principal thinks it's a good idea, you can work together to find someone to sponsor the game, and you can go from there. When I initially talked to the other sponsor, she would agree to play if they could host the game the following year. If football is a big deal in your area, you can assure them that they can make at least $800-$1000, and even more, if they have a concession stand.

- *Sign-up day*

Once everyone is in agreement (including the athletic director/head football coach), have a sign-up for varsity football players who want to coach. Once you've seen who has signed up, you can delegate who you want to be the head coach. He can then choose who he wants as his defensive coordinator, special teams coordinator, etc. There should also be a sign-up for cheerleaders. Warn them that they will be wearing skirts, wigs, and make-up, and will perform a short dance at halftime (more on cheerleaders later). You will also need three people to take care of the down markers. You may or may not have to coax your girls into playing. Have them sign up, and then if your best athletes aren't playing, find a way so they will! Be sure to make a team roster to hand out at the games once you've decided on positions.

- *Flags for the game*

Check with your physical education teachers for flag-football flags. There should be enough for BOTH teams to use. The first year we played, the other team came with their own flags which we thought were obviously harder to grab (they thought the same about ours), so both teams should wear the same kind of flags. There are guidelines in the rules on how to wear them properly.

- *Concessions*

I've done concession stands several times, and they are more of a pain than anything as far as I'm concerned. The most stress-free way to provide the fans with a concession stand is to let the pros take care of it. Whoever traditionally does the concessions at your school's regular home football games would be your best bet. Call whoever is in charge, and find out if they'll do it. They usually agree, but if not, check with another group in the school who might like to do it (e.g., student clubs, athletic boosters, student council, etc.).

- *Meet with the cheerleaders*

Have your school's actual cheerleaders take the group of young men who bravely signed up and transform them into polished cheerleaders. They should learn at least three cheers and a short dance routine for the pep rally and halftime show. Let your actual cheerleaders do all of the planning for the pep rally (signs, introductions of players, etc.) and for the game. The powder puff players will need a sign to run through as they come onto the field. The male cheerleaders are really the highlight of the whole game, so be sure they are dressed accordingly (wigs, make-up, etc.). Instead of trying to stuff big guys into cheerleading tops, have them wear their football jerseys with cheerleading skirts, so everyone knows who they are. If you choose, the jerseys will also give them plenty of room for strategically placed balloons.

- *Meeting with the other sponsor*

You'll need to meet with representatives of the other team to finalize rules and give them some flags so they can practice with them. Of course, be sure to count them so you get them all back. You know how those rival schools are. A set of rules needs to be agreed upon by both parties. (Refer to the sample set of rules that is included in the next section of this chapter). The game is designed to be an 11-on-11 game with kick-offs, returns, field goals, etc., which are not normally included in a traditional flag-football game.

Flag Football Rules

The Game: The playing rules for a powder puff football game are the same as those used for a regular high school game with the following exceptions:

- No rushing the kicker on an extra point attempt or a punt attempt
- A punted ball will be dead where it touches the ground, but not on a kickoff
- All players of the offensive team are eligible receivers
- Offensive blockers must have their hands clasped in front of themselves, as if setting a screen
- Defensive players are not allowed to push or pull offensive players
- Defensive players may not hold a ball carrier in order to grab the flag
- A player is considered down when her flag is pulled or if her flag falls off while in play

Equipment:

- Shirts or jerseys must be tucked in so flags are clearly visible and accessible
- A junior high football will be used by both teams
- Soccer type cleats may be worn and are recommended
- Both teams will agree on the type of flags to be worn

Organizing Practice

Finding a good practice time might be one of your more challenging tasks, since the male football players serving as the powder puff coaches are practicing hard for their own games, and your young women may or may not be involved in other activities. If you have a practice field with lights and the athletic director doesn't object, you could have practices there immediately after the the football team is through with it for the day. You can also practice in the gym (with appropriate shoes for the floor). Although it's tough in the gym, the girls can at least get practice running plays and grabbing flags. Saturday afternoons are really the best times to get everyone to practice. You'll have to be present at all practices, of course.

You'll need to give the individual who is serving as the head coach of your powder puff team some direction on what to do during practice and who to play. I considered myself the Jerry Jones of the entire operation because I wanted to win, and I didn't want anyone to be embarrassed on the field. That's not to say the coaches weren't competent, but since I had the training to be a coach, I was going to help. Once the game started, however, I let them call the plays. I just helped with personnel decisions and practice organization.

- *Personnel decisions*

  ❏ Find a quarterback. You will be most successful if you have someone who can throw the ball well. Use junior high footballs since they are smaller and easier to handle. The main emphasis of your offense should be passing the ball and using misdirection plays (e.g., reverses). But more on that later.

  ❏ Find out who can catch the ball. An easy way to do this is to get someone who can throw the ball (your new-found quarterback, if possible), line the players up, and have them run the routes that are illustrated in Figure C.1. Throw three to five passes at each route and have one of the coaches keep track of who makes a catch. Specify routes — some girls might catch an easy short slant pass, but have trouble with the long ball (if you have a quarterback that can throw the long ball, that is.)

- ❏ Find a center. You have to find someone who can snap the ball to the quarterback in a shotgun formation and then immediately block the player in front of her.

- ❏ Make your fastest four or five players your running backs. Because there won't be too any instances where your running backs will run right through the line, you want quickness to run sweeps and reverses.

- ❏ Put anyone who is aggressive and not afraid of contact on the line (defensive and offensive). This is usually a place for your slower athletes to play and do well.

- ❏ Find a place kicker and punter. Ask who wants to try, and have them work with a coach. They might need some instruction from your varsity kicker and punter on technique, but usually you will find a young woman who can just do it naturally.

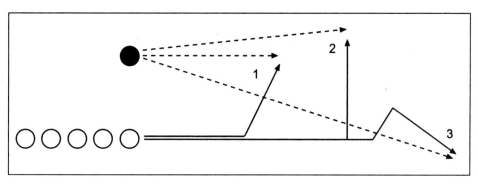

Figure C.1. Suggested passing routes.

- ❏ Put the rest of your players on special teams. If there are some girls who just want to be involved and are not athletically inclined, then they can be on the kick and kick-return team or the punt and punt-return team. They can also practice as backup o-line and d-line players. It's important to let everyone contribute, but still beat the "dog" out of the other team.

- ❏ Determine who will be your linebackers and secondary players. Linebackers stand just behind the defensive line and stop running backs, quarterbacks, and tight ends. The secondary players cover the receivers on pass plays and serve as a last line of defense on running plays. Because linebackers are generally quick players, use your running backs and quarterback in these positions. The particular defense we used had three linebackers (i.e., a 4-3), but your team might do something different. Players in the secondary need to be quick as well, but should know how to play man-to-man coverage. If they play basketball, this is easy. Your coaches will tell them what to do.

Drills For Practice

The first practice should be spent finding the right people for each position. After that first day, each young woman should know what position she will primarily play. As a result, when you start practice, everyone knows which coach to report to. The following drills are recommended, although your coaches could and will probably add others that they think would also be effective.

RUNNING BACKS

- *Ball-exchange drill* — Form two lines facing each other about six to eight yards apart; one player gets the ball. On command, the first players in each line starts running at the first player from the other line. When they meet, they execute an exchange of the ball, using the proper handoff technique. At that moment, the next player starts to get the next handoff, and then hands off the ball to the next player coming at them. Refer to Figure C.2.

- *Pitch drill* — Line up in a normal position behind the quarterback. Your precise positioning will be determined by specific plays designed by your coach. On a signal from the quarterback, receive the pitch in proper position and continue across the line of scrimmage. Get reps going both ways. Refer to Figure C.3.

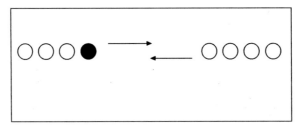

Figure C.2. Ball-exchange drill.

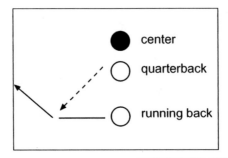

Figure C.3. Pitch drill.

QUARTERBACKS

- *Two-knees drills* (20 passes) — Pair off about 10 yards apart, directly in line with each other, while both of you are kneeling on both knees. The receiver will hold both of her hands up, giving the quarterback a target to throw to. Don't throw hard and concentrate on the target.

- *One-knee drill* (20 passes) — Put your knee on throwing side down. Place the ball on the ground, grip it with just your throwing hand, lift it up with one hand, cock it high with two hands, and throw to your drill partner. Exaggerate your follow-through.

- *Feet-parallel drill* (20 passes) — Pair off 12 yards apart, directly in line with each other. Increase the distance as you warm up. Don't exceed 20 yards and don't step with either foot.

- *Circle-toss drill* (three minutes) — Run in a circle, playing catch to simulate throwing on the run. Reverse the action.

- *Sprint-out drill* (20 passes) — Sprint right and left. Throw to another quarterback or to a specific target, making sure your shoulders and hips are square to target.

- *Individual-pass routes drill* — Throw to a receiver running any of the individual pass routes. This drill is designed to teach timing.

RECEIVERS

- *Quick-ball drill* — Players line up about 10 yards from the quarterback or coach. The drill begins by having the players run across the field at half speed, catching the ball, and then lining up on the other side. The drill can be repeated several times with variations on passes: low balls, high balls, and balls thrown behind the player. Refer to Figure C.4

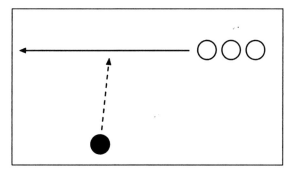

Figure C.4. Quick ball drill.

- *Tap-dance drill* — Players line up about 15 yards from the sideline. On command, the receiver starts to run three-quarter speed toward the sideline. The coach/quarterback will throw the ball about five yards from the sideline and the receiver will catch the ball and plant one foot inbounds before going out. Use drill on left and right side. See Figure C.5.

- *Turn-and-up drill* — Use the same procedure as the tap dance drill but the ball should be thrown seven to eight yards in front of the player so she can adjust and turn up field. See Figure C.6.

- *Route-tree drill* — A universal wide receiver route tree that you can use to run individual routes is illustrated in Figure C.7.

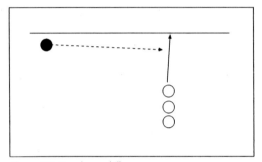

Figure C.5. Tap-dance drill.

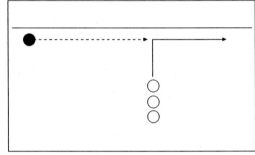

Figure C.6. Turn-and-up drill.

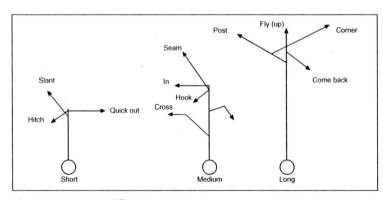

Figure C.7. Route-tree drill.

DEFENSIVE/OFFENSIVE LINE

Playing on the line is a tricky position because the rules govern how much contact can be made since no one is wearing pads or helmets. Both the offensive and defensive linewomen should get down in at least a three-point stance and then come up with their hands clasped in front of them similar to setting a screen in basketball. This requirement needs to be the case for both teams, since the center has to get down to snap the ball. Otherwise, she is at a great disadvantage, having to come up and block someone who is already in a standing position. Your boys can teach them what to do, whom to block, where to block, etc., according to the play.

LINEBACKERS

- *Flag-grabbing drill* — Two lines in front of each other about 10 yards apart. All players should be wearing flags. One player approaches the other, staying within a five-yard lane, while the other tries to grab the flag. Refer to Figure C.8.

- *Live-action drill* — While running backs are running the pitch drill, the linebackers can practice grabbing the flags.

- *Secondary drill* — While receivers run routes, the secondary can practice covering the receivers. Mix up routes.

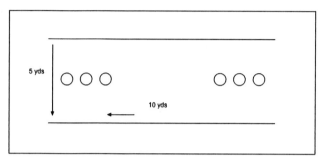

Figure C.8. Flag-grabbing drill.

The Playbook

The following list suggests a few plays that should work well. From past experience, any misdirection play you run should fool the defense, since most girls haven't been exposed to football very much. Also, passing the ball will be your best bet offensively if you've got the athletes to handle the demands of the passing game. Run these plays to the right or left.

- G.T. right (Refer to Figure C.9)
- G.T. right pass (Refer to Figure C.10)

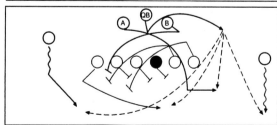

| Fake handoff to A, give to B and then roll out. | Played like GT Rt. except fake to A, fake to B, then look to pass. |

Figure C.9. G.T. right.   Figure C.10. G.T. right pass.

- Right, right, right (Refer to Figure C.11)
- Right, right, right pass (Refer to Figure C.12)

QB send B in motion then keeps the ball.

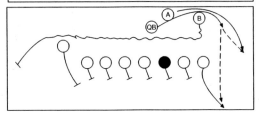

Figure C.11. Right, right, right.

QB sends B in motion, sprints out and looks to pass.

Figure C.12. Right, right, right pass.

- 48 sweep reverse (Refer to Figure C.13)
- 48 sweep reverse pass (Refer to Figure C.14)
- Trips (Refer to Figure C.15)

QB fakes handoff to A, then hands to Z. A should ben over and act like she has the ball.

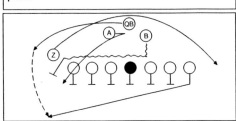

Figure C.13. 48 sweep reverse.

QB fakes handoff to A, fakes to Z, then rolls out for a pass.

Figure C.14. 48 sweep reverse pass.

A should be wide open. If A is covered, look to pass B1 or B2.

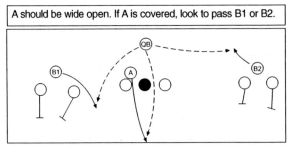

Figure C.15. Trips.

A Practice Outline (Six Practices)

- Practice #1 of six:

  - ❑ 60 minutes   Try-outs for positions

- Practice #2 of six:

  - ❑ 30 minutes   Individual-skills practice in groups (rotate after 15 minutes if a player plays more than one position)

  - ❑ 15 minutes   Extra-point practice

  - ❑ 15 minutes   Punt practice

- Practice #3 of six:

  - ❑ 20 minutes   Individual-skills practice (rotate in 10 min.)

  - ❑ 30 minutes   Practice the offense (learn plays using note cards)

  - ❑ 15 minutes   Punt-return practice

- Practice #4 of six:

  - ❑ 30 minutes   Offense vs. second-team defense

  - ❑ 20 minutes   Defense vs. second-team offense

  - ❑ 15 minutes   Kickoff practice

- Practice #5 of six:

  - ❑ 30 minutes   Defense vs. second-team offense

  - ❑ 20 minutes   Offense vs. second-team defense

  - ❑ 15 minutes   Kick-return practice

- Practice #6 of six:

  - ❑ Scrimmage vs. freshmen boys

You can obviously have more than six practices. If you have the time and energy, then by all means, increase the amount of time devoted to practicing. The kids really enjoy it. All factors being equal, playing and practicing the game will be fun no matter how many times you meet. Have the cheerleaders meet at the same time, so you don't have to go another time to cheerleading practices.

Preparations for Game Day

- ❏ Make sure the band will attend.
- ❏ Confirm availability of the concession stand.
- ❏ Get officials for the game.
- ❏ Hand out jerseys.
- ❏ Have a team meeting (coaches, cheerleaders, players, helpers).
- ❏ Get the down markers ready.
- ❏ Get an announcer and a person to videotape the game, including halftime.
- ❏ Publicize the event.

- *Band attendance*

The first year the band could not attend, so I had them make a tape of both the school song and the fight song and played it over the loudspeaker.

- *Officials for the game*

The first year we had two high school football coaches from each school who posed as officials. This worked out okay, but the impression I got was that they were afraid to make calls against the other team. The next year, we got intramural football officials from a nearby university. They, too, didn't make the tough calls, but did okay. You may try scheduling actual football officials who call junior high games and explain the rule changes. It's actually more like a real football game than an intramural flag-football game.

- *Jerseys for the girls*

Monday afternoon (the day before the game), you should hand out jerseys. Hopefully, your athletic director/head football coach will be cooperative. The first year, I asked the players what number they wanted and spent entirely too much time trying to accommodate them. So, the next year I just got 35 jerseys and handed them out, starting with the seniors, then the juniors, etc. If your athletes have workout shorts ,they can wear them for the game so everyone looks the same.

- *The big meeting*

Your coaches should dress alike for the game. It looks sharp and professional. Most of the time, varsity football players have a travel shirt they can wear with khaki pants. It just adds to the atmosphere. Have the coaches, cheerleaders, and powder-puff players wear their outfits to the meeting and take their pictures and then go over the game plan (when to be there, what to wear, etc.).

*   *Publicity*

Put ads in your local paper and post signs all over town to encourage attendance. Be sure to mention the cheerleaders, as some individuals will attend the game just to see male football players serving (and dressing) as cheerleaders. Make announcements at school and post signs in the opposing school's town, too.

GOLF TOURNAMENT

To a great degree, the amount of money you raise from this tournament depends on how much the golf course you use is going to charge you to let everyone play. I played in a tournament last winter and paid $50 to play. When it's to benefit a program at the school, it doesn't really matter to most people how much it costs. The $50 fee included the greens fee, cart, and awards. You could also purchase "mulligans" for $5 each (limit four). I'm not sure you could charge much more than $50 and still expect people to come out. Provide refreshments and give out T-shirts for all participants. The T-shirts are optional if funds won't allow the expense.

The format of the tournament should be a four-person scramble with a shotgun start (everyone starts at the same time but at different holes). Awards should go to the first-, second-, and third-place teams. Individual awards should be presented for longest drive and closest to the hole. You can give certificates for other awards, such as last place team, slice king/queen, and slowest team. Make up more if you feel so inclined.

Eight Weeks Before the Tournament

☐ Call the golf course, strike a deal (carts included), and set a date.

☐ Publicize the tournament at both the course and around town.

☐ Get entry forms out with all of the information.

☐ Line up volunteer helpers.

*   *Entry forms*

Find out who your potential golfers might be and get them a form as soon as possible. You'd like to have at least 10 teams. If a lot of interest exists, check with the golf course to see how many carts will be available. You may have to limit your tournament to a certain number of teams. Use the sample form illustrated in Figure C.16 as an entry form.

```
┌──────────────────────────────────────────────────────────────┐
│                  1st Annual Golf Tournament                    │
│                                                                │
│  WHEN:        April 24th, shotgun start at 8:00 a.m.           │
│                                                                │
│  WHERE:       Community Golf Course                            │
│                                                                │
│  FOR:         Taylor High School Girls' Athletics              │
│                                                                │
│  COST:        $50 per person (includes cart, greens fee, "goodie │
│               bag," and awards)                                │
│                                                                │
│  PRIZES:      $200 first prize, four Wilson golf bags, $100    │
│               longest drive, $100 closest to the pin, and others │
│                                                                │
│  Mulligans available for purchase on the day of the tournament ($5 │
│  each — limit two per person).                                 │
│                                                                │
│  Make checks payable to Anywhere H.S. and return the entry form │
│  and fee by March 30th to Coach Smith.                         │
│                                                                │
│  Team captain: _____ Number: _____           │
│                                                                │
│  Team members: _____                     │
│                                                                │
│                 _____                     │
│                                                                │
│                 _____                     │
│                                                                │
│  Entry fee:          _____  (# indiv's X $50 each)       │
│                      _____  (# of mulligans X $5 each)   │
│                                                                │
│  Amount of $ enclosed:  _____                            │
│                                                                │
└──────────────────────────────────────────────────────────────┘
```

Figure C.16. Sample golf-tournament entry form.

Four Weeks Before the Tournament

❏ Order plaques or trophies and T-shirts.

❏ Pay golf course required fees.

• *Order plaques and T-shirts*

The school may have someone with which it deals for plaques and trophies. Ask your athletic director who it is or if he has any product catalogues you might find useful. He also might have worked with a printer who will give you a relatively good deal on shirts. For example, the Little Dribbler's program, I was able to get good shirts for $4.25 each.

One Week Before the Tournament

- ❑ Get drinks.
- ❑ Pick up T-shirts and plaques.
- ❑ Make "farthest drive" and "closet to the pin" markers.
- ❑ Make poster to record all scores.

- *T-shirts*

Put a tag in each T-shirt with each participant's name and then alphabetize the T-shirts (by tags) to speed up handing them out when everyone is through.

- *Making the markers*

The markers should have a piece of paper with at least 10 lines for 10 names (more if the tournament is really large). Secure it to a piece of wire and stick it in the ground. At least one person from each team should have a pencil since they're keeping score.

- *The poster*

All you have to do is put team members' names in one column and leave a space for their score underneath. As each team finishes, record their scores on the board for everyone to see, as shown in Figure C.17.

John Smith Susan White Steve Scott Joe Garza	Sheryl Ham Lisa Porter Marge Frank Cindy Hall	Joseph Smith Danny Long Chris Lopez Al Johnson
72	69	75

Figure C.17. A sample scoreboard poster.

The Big Day

- ❑ Ice down the drinks.
- ❑ Put the markers out.
- ❑ Post the names of team members on the carts, along with the specific hole where they will start play.

- ❏ Arrange the plaques on a table.
- ❏ Set up a table for purchasing mulligans.
- ❏ Meet with everyone at 7:50 to get organized.

- *Putting the markers out*

Put the longest drive marker on a par-five hole that is somewhat wide open. The closest-to-the-hole marker should be placed on a short par three. Let teams know at the meeting which holes you've chosen.

When Everyone is Through

Once every team has finished, send someone out to pick up the markers and gather everyone for the awards presentation. Depending on the number of people who will be involved in the awards presentation, this can be extremely informal. If it's a large gathering, you may want to seat everyone in the clubhouse and use a podium for the presentations. Be sure to clean up all trash and park the carts in the appropriate place afterwards.

COED SOFTBALL TOURNAMENT

Use the same format for the golf tournament, with the following changes:

- ❏ Get permission to use the boys' baseball field.
- ❏ Go to neighboring towns and recreation centers to recruit teams.
- ❏ Charge at least $100 per team.
- ❏ Require each team to provide two softballs (check the size of the softballs).
- ❏ Hire three to four umpires.
- ❏ Get an official scorekeeper and clock/scoreboard keeper.
- ❏ Mail a bracket sheet to the coach in charge of each team.
- ❏ Organize a concession stand.
- ❏ Present T-shirts for the first-, second-, and third-place teams.

- *Using the baseball field*

A baseball field is more appropriate since it is a coed tournament. Technically, the fence should be between 275 ft. and 300 ft., and the bases should be moved to 60 ft. or 65 ft. instead of 90 ft. The pitching distance should be 46 ft., using a 12-inch ball. The day before the tournament, mark the baseline/foul lines and the batter's box. Each side of the plate should be a 3' x 7' rectangle.

- *Recruiting teams*

Go to neighboring grocery stores and churches to publicize the tournament. If you live in a larger city, you may have a city softball league where you can solicit teams during their games. Post a flyer in each dugout, and you will have plenty of teams interested.

- *Getting umpires*

If your baseball and softball coaches are not participating in the tournament, you could ask them to call the games for you. If they are playing (which will probably be the case), you can do one of two things. Either call the recreation center in your city and ask them for some names of umpires that call the city games, or call some umpires from the local baseball or softball chapter your school uses. Check to see what they usually earn for games and offer them the same level of compensation.

- *The bracket*

If you only have one field, it must have lights. The maximum number of teams you should allow is eight, which means a total of eleven games. Each game should have a time limit of 50 minutes, except the championship game. Each game is a seven-inning game with the normal run rule of 10 runs after five innings or 15 runs after four innings.

- *The scorekeeper, time keeper, and scoreboard keeper*

These jobs can be done by three people or just one. A scoreboard is not necessary, but a neutral scorekeeper and someone to keep the time for each game is important. This is a paid position as well, but could be done by the coaches who are helping you put on the tournament.

- *Concession stand*

If you can get someone to grill hamburgers, you can make quite a bit of additional money. Provide a meal that includes a hamburger, chips, and a drink for $3.00 or so. This will be especially successful if you are a small community without the convenience of a fast food option. Because most teams will be "stuck" at the field, and will pay almost anything for the food. Have bottled water available as well.

- *T-shirts*

For convenience, you could print one design for all the T-shirts rather than specifying first-, second-, or third-place. If it isn't a hassle with the printer, then distinguishing between them would obviously be better. Order at least 45 shirts (10 players and five subs per team).

- *Adhering to the scheduled time*

Stay as close to the schedule as possible so that the teams know when they will play. However, make each team aware that if a game ends unusually early, the next game will start immediately. Allow 10 minutes for a team to show and then call it a forfeit.

BASKETBALL-SKILLS DAY

This event has three-point, free-throw, and hot-shot contests and a 3-on-3 tournament. There are age groups for all events to make things fair. These events are designed for anyone seven to eighteen years old. The 3-on-3 tournament can have an additional division for older competitors (19 and older). If you think you will have a large turnout, then you can even separate the women from the men.

You can either finish this event on one Saturday or spread it out for two or three Saturdays depending on gym availability, helpers, and player interest. This event was very successful at Del Rio High School. In fact, the head men's basketball coach was expecting 50 kids and 300 showed up! Be sure to have a pre-registration, so you have an idea of how many individuals will be participating. Pre-registration will also allow you to fill out the 3-on-3 brackets and create a master list for the contests.

Six Weeks Before the Event

- ❏ Send a letter home with all second-grade through eighth-grade students.
- ❏ Begin announcing the event at the high school.
- ❏ Post signs around town and at school to promote the event.
- ❏ Decide upon the dates for registration.
- ❏ Order trophies or plaques.
- ❏ Recruit game monitors for scoring, concessions, etc.

- *Letter to prospects and registration form* – Refer to Figures C.18 and C.19.
- *Publicizing the event*

Post signs around town that include all of the important information and that note that registration forms can be picked up at (wherever) or will be made available at registration.

> Parents,
>
> *The G.H.S. Athletic Department will be hosting a Basketball Skills Event on May 8th, 15th & 22nd and would like to invite your son or daughter to participate. There will be a 3-pt. contest, a free-throw contest, and a hot-shot contest on the 8th and a 3-on-3 tournament starting on the 15th and finishing on the 22nd. The age divisions will be as follows:*
>
> *Boys: 3rd and 4th grade, 5th and 6th grade, 7th and 8th grade, 9th - 12th grade*
> *Girls: 3rd and 4th grade, 5th and 6th grade, 7th and 8th grade, 9th - 12th grade*
> *Men 19 and up, Women 19 and up & Coed 19 and up (3-on-3 tournament only)*
>
> *Fees for the event will be $10 for one shooting event ($25 for all three) and $30 per team for the 3-on-3 tournament.*
>
> *Registration will be held on April 24th and May 1st in the front foyer of the gym from 9:00 a.m. - 2:00 p.m.*
>
> *Please fill out the information sheet, sign the insurance waiver, and bring your check to registration. Late registration will be on May 8th from 8:00 a.m. - 8:45 a.m. and will be an additional $5 per event.*
>
> *Winners of each age division will receive a plaque for each contest and trophies will be awarded for first, second, and third place finishers in each age division for the 3-on-3 tournament. Everyone who registers by May 1st will receive a T-shirt for participation.*
>
> *Rules for the contests and tournament will be available at registration.*
>
> *Event times will be posted on May 3rd in front of the school.*

Figure C.18. Sample letter to prospective individuals who might be interested in participating.

- *Trophies and plaques*

Check in the "ordering awards" section of Appendix A for ordering guidelines. The number of trophies will depend on the level of participation. You may have to combine age groups for the 3-on-3 tournament, and, if so, will have to adjust this list accordingly. The number of plaques doesn't change, even if there's only one competitor in the division.

- Plaques (24 total)
  - ❑ Boys'/girls' third- and fourth-grade free-throw champion/three-point champion/hot-shot champion (six plaques)
  - ❑ Boys'/girls' fifth- and sixth-grade free-throw champion/three-point champion/hot-shot champion
  - ❑ Boys'/girls' seventh- and eighth-grade free-throw champion/three-point champion/hot-shot champion
  - ❑ Boys'/girls' high school free-throw champion/three-point champion/hot-shot champion

Basketball Skills Registration Form

Please fill out the following information and return, with your registration fee, to Stephenie Jordan on the following dates:

April 24th or May 1st from 9:00 a.m. - 2:00 p.m. in the main foyer of the gym.

Late registration will be from 8:00-8:45 a.m. on May 8th and will be an additional $5 per event.

The registration fees are as follows:

        $10 for each contest

        $25 for all three contests

        $30 per 3-on-3 team

Make checks payable to: Your school name or organization

Name of participant: _____ Male: ❑ Female: ❑

Check appropriate division: ❑ 3rd and 4th ❑ 5th and 6th ❑ 7th and 8th
                           ❑ 9th - 12th   ❑ 19 and up

Check events: ❑ Free throw contest   ❑ Three-point contest
                 ❑ Hot-shot contest   ❑ 3-on-3 team
                 ❑ Coed team

Circle T-shirt size: YS   YM   YL   S   M   L   XL   XXL
($2.00 extra)

Read carefully and sign the following insurance waiver:

I hereby give my consent for the above person to compete in the Basketball Skills Event. It is understood that although there is appropriate supervision, the possibility of an accident still remains. Neither the high school, coaches, nor other personnel assumes any responsibility in case an accident occurs. If, in the judgment of any representative of AHS, the above person needs immediate care and treatment as a result of an injury or sickness, I hereby request, authorize, and consent to such care and treatment as may be given to said child by any physician, trainer, nurse, or AHS representative. I do hereby agree to not sue and to release, indemnify, and hold harmless, the Anywhere I.S.D., its affiliates, officers, directors, volunteers, and employees from any and all liability, claims, demands, and causes of action whatsoever, arising out of my child's participation in this event and related activities.

I have read, understand, and agree to the terms of this Agreement.

Date: _____

Printed name of parent or guardian: _____

Signature of parent or guardian: _____

Figure C.19. Sample registration form.

- Trophies for tournament (99 total)

  - ❑ First place/second place/third place third- and fourth-grade boys'/girls' division (18 trophies — three per team)

  - ❑ First place/second place/third place fifth- and sixth-grade boys'/girls' division

  - ❑ First place/second place/third place seventh- and eighth-grade boys'/girls' division

  - ❑ First place/second place/third place ninth- through twelfth-grade boys'/girls' division

  - ❑ First place/second place/third place men's/women's/coed division (27 trophies)

- *Recruiting help*

You shouldn't have too much trouble recruiting help since this is a fund-raiser for your athletic program. Every member of the team (or every member in girls athletics) should be required to sign up to work. You'll need volunteers for the following:

- Check-in table — area for checking off the participants' names as they arrive. (two people)

- Scoring table — check out area for basketballs and pinnies, get scores, post scores in brackets, and keep games going on schedule. (three people)

- T-shirt table — have all T-shirts labeled with the participant's names, sorted alphabetically, ready to hand out. (two people)

- Trophies/plaques table — have all trophies and plaques arranged for easy distribution. (two people)

- Free-throw contest monitors — have the master list of participants, rules, and basketball at each of four baskets. (four people)

- Three-point contest monitors — have master list, rules, basketballs, and two helpers at each end basket. (two people)

- Three-point contest shaggers — help get the ball to the shooter. (four people)

- Hot-shot contest monitors — have the master list of participants, rules, basketball at each end basket; will need to mark spots on floor before contest. (two people)

- Three-on-three monitors* — keep score and "control" at each of four baskets. (four people) *The 3-on-3 monitors need to be adults and, if you have the extra cash, pay coaches or real officials to monitor the games. Agree to a set fee for the entire tournament.

- *Concessions*

Ask the seniors to provide a concession stand if they want to raise money for a graduation project (e.g., an after-graduation party). Agree to split the money however you feel is fair, (e.g., 30-70 maybe, since it is your event). It's up to you.

Four Weeks Before the Event

- ❏ Hold first of two registrations.
- ❏ Have rules ready for registration.
- ❏ Deposit money.

- *Registration day*

You'll need at least two tables and four helpers for registration. Split the tables up, with one for the 3-on-3 tournament and one for the three contests. To stay organized and to save time later, have manila envelopes clearly labeled for each division.

- *Contest table* (24 envelopes)
  - Boys'/girls' third- and fourth-grade free-throw/three-point/hot-shot contestants (six envelopes)
  - Boys'/Girls' fifth- and sixth-grade free-throw/three-point/hot-shot contestants
  - Boys'/girls' seventh- and eighth-grade free-throw/three-point/hot-shot contestants
  - Boys'/girls' high-school grade free-throw/three-point/hot-shot contestants

- *Tournament table* (11 envelopes)
  - Boys'/girls' third- and fourth-grade division (2 envelopes)
  - Boys'/girls' fifth- and sixth-grade division
  - Boys'/girls' seventh- and eighth-grade division
  - Boys'/girls' high-school division
  - Men's/women's/coed division (3 envelopes)

Money boxes, extra registration forms, copies of the rules, and pens should be at each table.

- *The rules*

❑ 3-on-3 tournament rules:

✓ Games are played on side goals and will last 10 minutes.

✓ Game monitors will keep game time, keep the score, call fouls, and resolve disputes.

✓ Regular basketball rules are used (e.g. fouls, travelling, etc.).

✓ The top team will wear pinnies.

✓ To start play, the team with the first possession starts at the top of the key and lets the opposing team "check" the ball. Once play begins, on each change of possession, teams must either dribble or pass the ball beyond the top of the key before a basket may be attempted.

✓ Scoring stays the same as with regulation basketball: two points for a field goal and three points for shots beyond the three-point line.

✓ If the team is coed, all members of the team must touch the ball before a basket can be counted.

✓ No substitutes are allowed. If a member of the team is injured and cannot continue, the team must forfeit.

- Free-throw shooting

Each participant will take 25 shots from the regulation free-throw line and will shoot at a 10-foot goal. If a tie occurs, the finalists will take five additional shots until a winner is declared.

- Three-point shooting

The participants will take 15 shots from beyond the three-point line and will shoot at a 10-foot goal. If a tie occurs, the finalists will take three additional shots until a winner is declared.

- Hot-shot shooting

Each participant is given two minutes to score as many baskets as possible. The shooter starts at the top of the key, and on the signal, begins shooting. Participants are responsible for their own rebounds, and a referee keeps score. The scoring is as illustrated in Figure C.20. If the participant shoots from each position: five points extra. If the participant makes a shot from each position: 10 points extra.

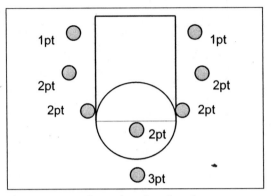

Figure C.20. Sample area-based scoring scheme.

Two Weeks Before the Event

❑ Hold a second registration.

❑ Order T-shirts.

• *Ordering T-shirts*

After the second registration, you will know exactly how many T-shirts you will need. Those who register late should not receive a T-shirt, a stipulation which is noted in the information sheet on the event.

One Week Before the Event

❑ Determine a format for the tournament.

❑ Make master list for each contest and 3-on-3 teams.

❑ Fill in brackets for 3-on-3.

❑ Post times for contests and tournament.

❑ Acquire and organize pinnies.

• *Tournament format*

The format will be determined by the number of teams that sign up. The following three types of tournament formats should be considered:

- ❏ Round robin — Every team plays every other team; the team that wins the most games is the tournament champion. If two or more teams tie for first place, the winner is selected on the basis of the total points of all the games played. Used for a small turnout.
- ❏ Double elimination — The winners of the first round are placed in bracket A, while those that lose are placed in bracket B. Eventually, the winner of bracket B plays the winner of bracket A and must defeat them twice to win.
- ❏ Single elimination — The winners advance to the next round while losers are eliminated.

- *Master lists*

As soon as you have the second and final registration, you need to list every participant on a master list. These lists should be at the check-in table and then given to the contest monitors at the start of the event. Use the sample form illustrated in Figure C.21 to make your master lists.

3rd- and 4th-Grade Girls' Free-Throw Participants			
No.	Name	T-shirt	Total # of F.T.'s
1	Adkison, Susie	YM	
2	Calhoun, Jane	YL	
3	Daniels, Tina	M	
4	Miller, Laura	YM	
5	Reneau, Amy	YL	
6	Ross, Diana	YM	
7	Walker, Faith	YL	

Figure C.21. Sample form for recording master list.

- *Fill in the brackets*

After you decide a tournament format, fill in each bracket and post it so the teams will know the time schedule. Allow 15 minutes for each game in order to stay on schedule. Remember, each game is 10 minutes long. If you have a large turnout and access to two gyms, you can really get things rolling. A sample bracket for a single elimination format is illustrated in Figure C.22. You'll have 11 brackets when you're through.

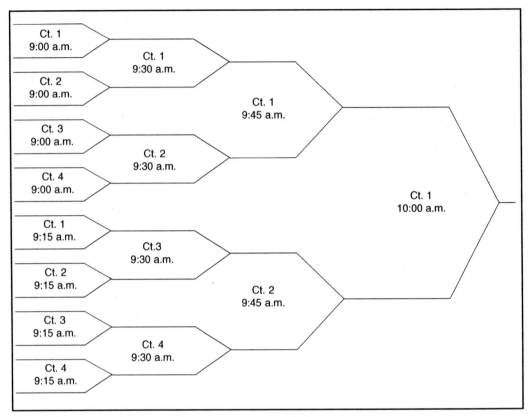

Figure C.22. Sample single-elimination tournament bracket for a 16-team tournament.

- *Post times and brackets:*

❏ **Saturday #1**

8:00 a.m.	Late registration and check-in
9:00 a.m.	Third- and fourth-grade free-throw contest
9:30 a.m.	Third- and fourth-grade three-point contest
10:15 a.m.	Third- and fourth-grade hot-shot contest
11:00 a.m.	Fifth- and sixth-grade free-throw contest
11:30 a.m.	Fifth- and sixth-grade three-point contest
12:15 p.m.	Fifth- and sixth-grade hot-shot contest
1:00 p.m.	Clear gym and break for lunch (or use time to get back on schedule)
1:30 p.m.	Seventh- and eighth-grade free-throw contest

2:00 p.m.	Seventh- and eighth-grade three-point contest
2:45 p.m.	Seventh- and eighth-grade hot-shot contest
3:30 p.m.	High-school free-throw contest
4:00 p.m.	High-school three-point contest
4:45 p.m.	High-school hot-shot contest

❑ Saturday #2 and #3

The schedule on these two days will be determined by the number of teams entered in the event. Start the youngest division at 9:00 a.m. and go from there.

The Day Before the Event

- ❑ Get sound system ready (optional).
- ❑ Meet with all workers once more (stress being early — 8:00 a.m.).
- ❑ Set up tables for check-in, late registration, and score reporting.
- ❑ Have plenty of basketballs ready.
- ❑ Mark the floor for the hot-shot competition (with tape).
- ❑ Post signs by the baskets.

- *Signs*

Post signs for each age group so they know where they need to be.

The Day of the Event

- ❑ Check participants off the master sign-up sheet as they arrive and hand out T-shirts at that time.
- ❑ Issue teams a basketball.
- ❑ Before play begins, welcome all participants and explain rules and procedures.

Schedule of Events

Once the program actually begins, a number of events will occur, including late registration and check-in, the free-throw contest, the three-point contest, the hot-shot contest, and the 3-on-3 tournament.

- Late registration and check-in

Don't open the gym until 8:45 a.m., so you don't have to baby-sit. Contest monitors should set up their stations by posting their signs and getting a clipboard and pencil ready.

- Free-throw contest

Set the game clock for 15 minutes after you open the doors so kids can shoot. When the buzzer goes off, bring everyone to the center of the court and explain the rules of the event. Send the kids to their appropriate basket, and have the first contestant step up to the line. The rest of the kids should sit quietly out of the way in the order they will be shooting. Once each participant has shot 25 times, determine if playoffs are needed. Immediately award a plaque to the winner. If a particular station ends sooner than the others, send the kids out of the gym so they are not a distraction to the other participants.

- Three-point contest

Each participant shoots 15 times at the end goals, while others sit and watch. The monitors should have two helpers to rebound balls for the shooter to speed things up. Have at least five balls at each basket. Kids who sign up for the three-point contest who cannot shoot that far will not be allowed to move closer. It wouldn't be a three-point contest then, would it? Award the plaque immediately after the contest.

- Hot-shot contest

This contest is also conducted at the end baskets that have been previously marked. This event is timed, so both contests should finish together. Use the game clock so the monitors can keep up with the point totals. The monitor should have a diagram for each child, so all that is needed is to put tally marks in each circle and to keep track of bonus points (five extra for shooting at each spot and 10 extra for making a basket from each spot). Have a helper tally points as each participant finishes, so things will keep rolling and a winner can be declared immediately following the event.

- 3-on-3 tournament

As teams check in, they should get a copy of the tournament bracket, so they know when and where they play. Each monitor should have a bracket, pencil, three pinnies, and a basketball. When a game finishes, the monitor posts the score on the master bracket on the wall.

OTHER FUND-RAISING IDEAS

- Garage sale – Use items donated by community members.

- Spaghetti supper – Get merchants to donate ingredients and have the dinner before a home football game.

- Potluck supper – Have parents of players bring dishes for the supper and have a set charge per plate. Seconds are allowed, but individuals could be charged for another plate. Conduct an auction of different items in conjunction with the supper, such as old uniforms, cakes, and pies.

- Road race – This can be similar to a cross-country meet. Give participants T-shirts and prizes for winners in each age division (you decide on the age groups).

- Baked potato supper – Again, try to get food donated and include different toppings such as chopped meat, nacho cheese, etc.

Stephenie Jordan earned her bachelor of science degree in mathematics from Southwest Texas State University, with a minor in physical education. With the Bobcats, she earned varsity letters in volleyball and track & field and was a two-time Southland Conference Champion and a school record holder in the heptathlon. Before attending SWTSU, she was recruited to Western Illinois University as a freshman pentathlete/heptathlete and was selected all-conference in the javelin for the Gateway Collegiate Athletic Conference. She also earned a varsity letter for volleyball for the Westerwinds.

During her high school athletic career, Stephenie won varsity letters in volleyball, basketball, tennis, and track & field at O'Fallon Township High School. She qualified for the state track meet in the discus and 300-meter hurdles, played on the number one doubles team in tennis, and was named her school's Athlete of the Year in 1987.

She began her coaching career in the summer of 1991 at Camp Ozark, where she was the head coach for all team competitions and later became the girls' sports director in 1993. Her first teaching job was at Bellville Junior High School, in Bellville, Texas, where she coached seventh-grade girls. She assisted the varsity Brahmanette volleyball team to a 3A state title in 1993 and to the state finals in 1994. Also, at Bellville, Stephenie was the J.V. volleyball coach, the J.V. basketball coach, an assistant varsity track coach, the J.V. cheerleading sponsor, and the director of Fellowship of Christian Athletes. She also served as the tournament director of the 47th Annual Basketball Tournament and helped supervise the Little Dribbler's program.

Next, Stephenie accepted a teaching and coaching position in Arp, Texas. In that position, she was the head track coach when 14 out of 16 young women on the squad qualified to compete beyond the district meet. In addition, she assisted the volleyball team as they advanced to the area finals, coached the J.V. and freshman volleyball teams, and again sponsored the Fellowship of Christian Athletes.

The following year Stephenie became the first softball coach ever at Garrison High School in Garrison, Texas. In her squad's first season, the team went 8-4 and played in the first round of the state playoffs. She also coached the junior high girls' basketball teams, assisted the varsity team, coached the boys' and girls' cross-country teams, served as the Little Dribbler's Program Coordinator for two years, coached two high jumpers to the regional finals, and sponsored the Fellowship of Christian Athletes.

Stephenie and her husband, Jody, have a son, Scott, and a daughter, Rebekah. She has temporarily given up full-time coaching to raise their family in Point, Texas.